Our
Pentecostal
Heritage

Reclaiming
the Priority
of the Holy Spirit

Our
Pentecostal
Heritage

John A. Sims

Pathway
CLEVELAND, TENNESSEE 37311

Library of Congress
Catalog Card Number: 95-069982
ISBN: 871486733
Copyright © 1995 by Pathway Press
Cleveland, Tennessee 37311
All Rights Reserved
Printed in the United States of America

Affectionately dedicated to my colleagues at Lee College, friends with whom I have been privileged to do Kingdom work for the past 25 years.

Contents

Pentecostal Spirituality
Commitment to the Unity of Word and Spirit
A Latter Rain Movement
A Christ-centered Spirituality

A Bold and Courageous Faith
Ministering in the Power of the Holy Spirit
   Through a Worshiping Church
   Through a Learning Church
   Through a Unified Church

Institutional Structures
Love and Service
An Inclusive Community

Doctrine of Salvation
Justification and Regeneration
Entire Sanctification
Rise of the Holiness Movement
Divine Healing Provided in the Atonement
Pentecostal Eschatology
Premillenial Second Coming of Christ

Preface

The making of a book is a task that involves many people. There are those who inspire it, those who encourage and stand by the author during the writing process, and those who actually put the book together. I would like to take this opportunity to thank all of those who fit into one or more of these categories.

Virtually all of us who consider ourselves a part of the Pentecostal tradition acknowledge with gratitude and appreciation those who have inspired and shaped our heritage through precept and godly example. They are the reason and the inspiration for the heritage we share.

The idea for this book was conceived in collaboration with my colleagues in the Department of Bible and Christian Ministries at Lee College. We were concerned that too many students were passing through our courses without an adequate introduction to our Pentecostal heritage. We wanted a book that could be used in our Christian Thought course that would at least introduce students to the rudiments of the tradition.

A special acknowledgment is due our department chairman, Dr. Jerald Daffe, who encouraged the project from the beginning, and to other colleagues who read the manuscript and offered valuable insight and advice. A special debt of gratitude is owed to the publishers at Pathway Press, especially Homer G. Rhea and Marcus V. Hand, who have been encouraging and helpful in every stage of the publishing process. As always, my wife, Pat, has been my best friend and supporter, and I am especially grateful to her for enduring love, support, and encouragement.

I trust that this book will help fill a need among those who would like to know more about their Pentecostal heritage. No religious movement is more than one generation removed from extinction. All of our students need to know, in a personal way, the power and purpose of Pentecost.

A hundred years have passed since the outpouring of the Holy Spirit on our Pentecostal forebears at Shearer Schoolhouse in North Carolina. As we reflect on and celebrate our Pentecostal heritage, I trust that this small volume will kindle a greater appreciation for the movement and its commitments. That would make all the efforts in producing it worthwhile. Also, to those who are familiar with the Pentecostal Movement but would like to know more about its past, this volume is offered to them. I hope they too can come to a greater appreciation for the movement and share in the blessings of Pentecost.

John A. Sims, Ph.D.
Professor of Religion and History
Lee College

SMALL
BEGINNINGS

During the two-year period between 1884 and 1886, Richard G. Spurling; his son, Richard Spurling, Jr.; and John Plemons studied Scriptures and prayed earnestly for the spiritual condition of the Baptist church they attended. However, their passion for revival and reform was not shared by many other people in their mountain community on the border of North Carolina and Tennessee.

In late summer 1886, the three met at Barney Creek Meetinghouse with a few neighbors who did share their eagerness for spiritual renewal. The older Spurling addressed the gathering. He spoke with earnestness and enthusiasm about the divine guidance he believed had brought the small group together. He exhorted them to seek spiritual renewal. Then he urged them to form a Christian union that would reassert the authority of the Scriptures, foster Christian unity in the community, and restore the spiritual life of primitive Christianity.

When Spurling finished speaking, he invited those present to join in Christian union. Spurling's invitation was brief and to the point:

As many Christians as are here present that are desirous to be free from all man-made creeds and traditions, and are willing to take the New Testament, or law of Christ, for your only rule of faith and practice; giving each other equal rights and privilege to read and interpret for yourselves as your conscience may dictate, and are willing to sit together as the Church of God to transact business as the same, come forward.[1]

Before the day was through, nine individuals had stepped forward to accept Spurling's invitation. In a business session the small group decided to call itself Christian Union. They selected Richard G. Spurling as minister of the small but zealous congregation. They sensed that what was happening was not a mere coincidence; they felt that somehow the Holy Spirit had gathered them for a special purpose. Spurling's first act as pastor was to pray a pastoral prayer, committing the small body to the will of Christ and asking God's "guidance and blessing upon the group that it might grow and prosper and accomplish great good."[2] No one present that day could have possibly imagined the full extent to which God would answer that prayer.

In its formative beginning the young church was distinguished more by its passion for a deeper spiritual walk with God than by a specific doctrine or practice. A deep-seated conviction compelled the group to continue to seek God for spiritual revival and reform. They were specifically concerned about the spiritual and moral laxity in the churches and in the community. Those who joined Christian Union were weary of traditional churches where there was no felt presence of God, where so-called conversions did not result in moral and spiritual transformation, and where there was neither holiness of life nor true spiritual worship.

What the Barney Creek believers hungered for, however, did not come until 10 years later when a revival broke out at Shearer Schoolhouse near Camp Creek, North Carolina. During this revival their spiritual discontent was turned into a positive experience with God. Three visiting evangelists—William Martin, Joe Tipton, and Milton McNabb—preached on the joys of a transformed and sanctified life. Night after night the altars filled with seekers hungry for the experience of sanctification. Mountain folk from near and far crowded the one-room schoolhouse in search of a closer walk with God.

Simple services conducted in a moving manner set a tone for spiritual worship that would characterize these holiness believers and their descendants for generations to come. Music was often without instrumental accompaniment. They punctuated the singing of well-known hymns with testimonies and concert prayer. One of the evangelists preached the climactic sermon and invited seekers to extended periods of prayer around a makeshift altar.

The meetings were unconventional. Unusual things happened at Camp Creek. Worshipers expressed the felt presence of God through weeping, shouting, and unusual forms of spiritual ecstasy. Dancing in the Spirit and trances were common. When the surrounding community began hearing of healings and of unknown tongues, even the Camp Creek believers did not know how to explain them.³ They turned to the New Testament for answers, however, and discovered there the same power and presence of the Holy Spirit they were experiencing.

Luke tells us in Acts 2 that when the Holy Spirit was poured out on the church at Pentecost, unusual signs occurred. Those filled with the Holy Spirit began to speak in other tongues as the Spirit gave them the utterance. These Spirit-filled believers did not remain in the Upper Room but went immediately into the city of Jerusalem, where foreigners from every nation present heard them praising God for His mighty deeds of power in their own languages. It was such a strange and unexplainable phenomenon that perplexed bystanders asked, "What does this mean?"

Similar things occurred among the holiness believers in the Camp Creek community. Friends and neighbors asked what it all meant. Many who had "prayed through" to the sanctification experience at Camp Creek spoke in "other tongues" and were themselves perplexed by the strange phenomenon they had experienced.

The community's curiosity to this "tongues experience" and to the emotionalism of the meeting soon turned negative and violent. Before the revival ended, several homes had been pillaged and burned. Even religious leaders in the community as well as the local sheriff took part in the persecution of the small band of believers. They were forced to move from the schoolhouse. In the home of W.F. Bryant, one of the members, Spurling continued to provide spiritual leadership for the group.

The determined group managed to stay together, and in 1902 they reorganized under the name "The Holiness Church at Camp Creek." In 1903 A.J. Tomlinson, an itinerant preacher and Bible salesman from Indiana, joined the group and soon took the reins of leadership in the growing and expanding movement.

Other congregations sprang up and were organized throughout the region. In 1906 these churches came together in Cherokee County, North Carolina, for their first General Assembly.[4] At the Second General Assembly the next year, the churches officially changed their name to the Church of God.[5] Tomlinson provided strong and vigorous leadership in the early years of the movement. In 1909 he was elected to fill the church's first executive office as general overseer. By this time the center of the church's activities had shifted westward, across the mountains, to Cleveland, Tennessee, which was destined to become the international headquarters for the church.

The year 1910 was important for the young church. Church of God missionaries went to a foreign country for the first time—the Bahama Islands. That same year the church published its first denominational journal, *The Evening Light and Church of God Evangel*. The church also codified its teachings for the first time.

As the young church grew and prospered, so did its need for organizational structures that could facilitate and promote the growth the church was experiencing. In 1911 state overseers were appointed to supervise the work of the church throughout the southeastern region of the United States. In 1916 a council of 12 men was created to oversee the affairs of the church between General Assemblies. The following year the church began operating its own publishing plant in order to publish Sunday school materials and other publications. In 1918, in the midst of World War I and an influenza epidemic, a teacher named Nora Chambers began offering the first classes in a Bible Training Center that would eventually be known as Lee College. The church felt a burden to care for neglected and orphaned children and in 1920 established its first Home for Children.

By the close of the decade of the '20s, most of the necessary institutional structures had been put in place, and international expansion of the church began in earnest. Missions enterprise was greatly enhanced by the formation of a Missions Board in 1926. By 1966, Church of God membership outside the United States exceeded that in this country. Meanwhile, the church continued to add educational institutions for the training of ministers and Christian workers.[6]

The growing church began strengthening its bonds with other Evangelical and Pentecostal groups. In 1942 the Church of God joined other Evangelicals in forming the National Association of Evangelicals (NAE), and in 1948 it participated in the formation of the Pentecostal Fellowship of North America (PFNA). In that same year the church authorized and adopted an official Declaration of Faith.

In the early years of the 20th century, Church of God members had no concept of the magnitude of the Pentecostal revival of which they were a part.

They knew something special had happened to them and were eager to share the joys of their newfound experience, but little did they know that the Holy Spirit was being poured out simultaneously on believers throughout the United States and around the world. In the absence of a clearly articulated doctrine regarding the baptism in the Holy Spirit, the church did little to publicly proclaim the experience until after news of the Azusa Street outpouring began spreading around the world. From 1906 forward, the Church of God became a full-fledged Pentecostal church and began to publicly proclaim and publish the Pentecostal doctrine.

Pentecostal Spirituality

Early Pentecostals were ardently concerned about sound doctrine and institutional structures, but neither was their primary concern. What was important to them was their experience of the presence and power of the Holy Spirit in their lives and the conviction that the Holy Spirit was repeating what He had done in the apostolic church.

Pentecostals were committed Christians who hungered for God's spiritual presence. Spirituality to them was not a buzzword. It was not some technique or feel-good experience giving intimacy with the living God apart from the spiritual disciplines of prayer, obedience, and a full life commitment.[7] They understood that true spirituality is not a fad but a way of life that is grounded in eternal truth. In the knowledge and spirit of this wisdom, early Pentecostals premised their spirituality on solid formative principles.

Commitment to the Unity of Word and Spirit

For Pentecostals, orthodox theology, experience, and practice begins in Scripture as Christian truth. Truth about God, His purposes, and how He seeks to relate to us is not a matter of human discovery but of divine disclosure in Holy Writ. This is the bedrock foundation upon which legitimate spirituality must rest.

Pentecostal spirituality was grounded in biblical authority from the onset of the movement. The first article of faith established at the first General Assembly of the Church of God was "The New Testament is our only rule of faith and practice." The first article of the Declaration of Faith in 1948 stated: "We believe in the verbal inspiration of the Bible." These statements affirmed in the strongest possible terms the church's belief that Scripture is infallible in all it says and teaches. The Spirit of God, who spoke through the prophets and apostles to give us the written Word, is the sole authority for Christian truth. This written Word, contained in the 66 canonical books comprising the Protestant Bible, is the norm by which all claims to experience, reason, and tradition are tested and judged.

Pentecostals are unequivocal in their conviction that spiritual experience must always be critiqued by objective norms of Scripture. Yet they also believe a viable theology cannot be devoid of meaningful experience. Theology that is not confirmed by authentic religious experience is not likely to have much vitality or staying power.[8] The truths of evangelical faith may remain true and unshakable but still lack vitality. What we know intellectually may be doing little to shape our lives. Unless truths are authenticated and set aflame by the Holy Spirit, they generate no spiritual power or effective witness.

What God reveals to us in Scripture contains mental communications indispensable to the Christian life. The Bible emphasizes more than what one can know *about* God. Through the agency of the Holy Spirit, it seeks to introduce us to God.

Paul wrote in 2 Timothy 1:12, "I know whom I have believed." The work of the Spirit always presupposes the revelation given in Scripture and serves to prepare hearts to respond to and embrace the Word. The Word is authenticated in those who are empowered by the Spirit to perceive this authentication. Sugar is sweet whether we taste it or not. Its sweetness is authenticated only to those who are able to taste it. Blue is blue regardless of the trustworthiness of our own sight. Yet the color blue is only authenticated for those who can see blue.

John Calvin, the Protestant reformer, spoke of this necessary correlation between objective and subjective dimensions of biblical authority. In his *Institutes of the Christian Religion* he wrote:

> The Word itself has not much certainty with us, unless when confirmed by the testimony of the Spirit. For the Lord has established a kind of mutual connection between the certainty of His Word and of His Spirit; so that our minds are filled with a solid reverence for the Word when by the light of the Spirit we are enabled to behold the face of God; and on the other hand, we gladly receive the Spirit when we recognize Him in His image, that is, in the Word.[9]

The Holy Spirit works, then, in two ways. He works externally through the inspired written Word;

He works internally as the illuminating and convincing Spirit. The majesty of God is in His Word, but we do not see that majesty unless the Holy Spirit shows it to us. The living witness of the Spirit is a safeguard against the danger of scriptural authoritarianism, while the objective truth of the revealed Word guards against the excesses of subjectivity.[10]

Pentecostal spirituality holds that genuine faith must always be a personal activity. The Holy Spirit does not introduce us to an abstract "it" but to a personal "Thou." The highest form of knowing God is "knowledge by acquaintance." They know Him best who have personal fellowship and communion with Christ through the agency of the Holy Spirit.

The authority of the written Word can never be rightly contradicted or superseded, for the prophets and apostles who brought us the written Word were exercised by the inspiration of the Holy Spirit in a special and unique manner. This does not mean that the Spirit of God no longer speaks to the people of God. At the heart of Pentecostal worship is a sense of living in the presence of the Holy Spirit and being led by that same Spirit. Steve Land, a Pentecostal theologian, alludes to this vital interaction of Word and Spirit:

> Experience is vital in knowing the truth, for truth is not merely propositional—it is personal ("He who does not love does not know God," 1 John 4:8). . . . Therefore, in Pentecostal spirituality there is a coming together to hear our testimonies, to hear the testimony of Scripture, to wait for the Spirit's critical call to action-application, and then to yield to His leading. As Pentecostals act on the Word and walk in the light, they have fellowship and are (as the

Scriptures promise) cleansed from all unrighteous-
ness.[11]

French Arrington, a Pentecostal Bible scholar, elaborates further on the manner in which Pentecostals
have traditionally approached the interpretation of
Scripture:

> Pentecostals see knowledge not as a cognitive recog-
> nition of a set of precepts but as a relationship with
> the One who has established the precepts by which
> we live. The teachings of Scripture remain ambigu-
> ous until the Holy Spirit, who searches even the
> deep things of God (1 Corinthians 2:10), illuminates
> human understanding to the mysteries of the
> Gospel, but such a pneumatic epistemology finds its
> roots in the Scripture itself. Thus the believer knows
> God as Adam knew Eve, and he comes to know God
> through his Christian walk in fellowship with the
> Spirit. His belief then is not merely an intellectual
> acceptance of precepts but is a lived response to his
> lived relationship with the Spirit of God. As a result,
> the believer comes to understand the Word of God
> only in his relationship with its ultimate author, the
> Spirit of God.[12]

A Latter Rain Movement

Another premise underlying Pentecostal spirituality is the eschatological dimension underscoring the
urgency of the Pentecostal mission. This term is
from the Greek word *eschaton*, which means "last
things." Pentecostals believe that the outpouring of
the Holy Spirit upon the church in these latter times
has been for the purpose of preparing the church for
the soon return of Jesus Christ.

The New Testament uses two words for "time."

The first is *chronos*, from which we get our English word *chronology*. It is essentially a quantitative term, denoting a sequential ordering of events. The other word is *kairos*, a qualitative term denoting a special moment, a spiritual breakthrough, in which the divine presence accomplishes some special purpose of God.

The biblical significance of such a moment is explained by Paul Tillich, a modern theologian:

> Awareness of a *kairos* is a matter of vision. It is not an object of analysis and calculation such as could be given in psychological or sociological terms. It is not a matter of detached observation but of involved experience. This, however, does not mean that observation and analysis are excluded; they serve to objectify the experience and to clarify and enrich the vision. But observation and analysis do not produce the experience of the *kairos*. The prophetic Spirit works creatively without any dependence on argumentation and goodwill. But every moment which claims to be spiritual must be tested, and the criterion is the great *kairos*.[13]

There have been many such moments (*kairoi*) in biblical and postbiblical times. Both John the Baptist and Jesus announced a fulfillment of time with regard to the kingdom of God, which they said was "at hand." Paul spoke about the fullness of time (*kairos*) when God sent His Son to redeem those under the bondage of the law (Galatians 4:4). There was a time (*kairos*) for Christ's coming, His ministry, suffering, death, and resurrection from the dead. There will also be a time for His return.

Kairos experiences, as well as biblical events, are a part of the history of the church. In both history and

Scripture the divine presence and the Kingdom have broken through in special manifestations. Although church history records relatively long periods when the prophetic Spirit was seemingly latent or hindered by human tradition, the kingdom of God has never been totally absent. All claims to a *kairos* experience, however, have to be tested, as Tillich suggests, by the criterion of "the great *kairos*," which is Christ and His gospel.

At the turn of the 20th century, the Holy Spirit was poured out anew upon believers at Camp Creek; in Topeka, Kansas; at Azusa Street; and in various places around the world. Those receiving this experience were convinced of a special spiritual breakthrough meant to empower them to fulfill a special purpose in the last days. Modern Pentecost was, they believed, a "latter rain" movement intended to prepare the church for the second coming of Christ.

This conviction, more than any other, gave modern Pentecostals their sense of self-identity. The great spiritual moment they were experiencing was not some form of aberrant belief or behavior; it was a divinely ordained move of the Holy Spirit. What God was doing in them was obviously related to what God had begun on the Day of Pentecost, as recorded in Acts 2. Pentecostals were not disconnected from classical forms of Christianity, as some would suggest, but were directly related to the end-time fulfillment of what God had begun in the apostolic church.

The image of the latter rain doctrine is derived from the two major seasons of rainfall in Palestine. The first came in the fall and prepared the soil for planting. This "former rain," Pentecostals believed, corresponded to the first Pentecost (Acts 2), which initiated the work of the church, the great planting of the gospel. After the apostolic era, however, the church experienced a great drought of the Spirit. It lost much of its force and power as Rome institutionalized and sacramentalized virtually all spiritual activity.

In Palestine the latter rain occurred in the spring of the year. It ripened the crops for harvest. Pentecostals believed this corresponded to the outpouring of the Holy Spirit in the 20th century for the purpose of renewing the church and preparing the world (that is, the harvest) for the imminent return of Jesus Christ. Gifts and miracles reappeared in an extraordinary manner, they believed, because God was equipping the church to gather the harvest of the last days. These beliefs clearly defined the church's agenda of evangelizing the world and preparing the church for the return of Christ.

A Christ-centered Spirituality

The Protestant Bible contains 66 books with two major divisions, the Old and the New Testaments. A common theme brings all the diversity of the Scriptures into a magnificent unity. That common theme is God and His purpose as revealed in Jesus Christ. Creation, the Fall, the promise and prophecy, the coming of Christ in the fullness of time, His life and death, the Resurrection and the Ascension, the coming of the Holy Spirit, the church, the proclamation of the gospel, the Second Coming, and the final consummation are all directly related to this central truth.

Contrary to what many suppose, Pentecostal spirituality is not centered in the Holy Spirit but in Jesus Christ. Christian doctrine and experience find their focus in Him. Every legitimate manifestation of the Spirit's power and presence in the church today must meet the criterion of His manifestation in Jesus as the Christ. All theologies of experience have the Christ-character of Jesus (that is, the presence of the Spirit in Jesus) as their critic. All forms of piety that do not conform to the Christocentric model are, in one way or another, distorted.

Pentecostals were traditionally drawn to the narrative texts of the synoptic writers (especially Luke) and the Book of Acts, which record the pattern of the Spirit's presence and activity in the life and ministry of Christ and in the early church. In these texts they discovered the spiritual presence that possessed Christ's being and energized His human spirit. The meaning they drew from these narratives was that Christ's life and mission were not meant to be isolated events. Rather, they are key to understanding all true spiritual manifestations in the history of the church.

An organic relationship exists between the Spirit's past activity in Jesus and the subsequent activity of the Spirit in the life of the church. The hermeneutical principle that Pentecostals have always followed in the appropriation of Scripture was that Jesus' life and ministry were meant to be programmatic. His life in the Spirit comprised a normative plan of action for their own.[14] As Spirit-filled Christians they must continue the mission of Jesus Christ in the world through the power and presence of the Holy Spirit.

The basis for this Spirit-Christology begins in the Old Testament. The hope of Israel was a messianic age, a time when there would be a great outpouring of the prophetic Spirit upon the Messiah and all the people of Israel. It was expected that the Spirit of God would rest upon the Messiah in a special way and equip Him for the messianic task. As Isaiah prophesied, "The Spirit of the Lord shall rest upon Him" (Isaiah 11:2, see also 61:1). Joel prophesied that the Spirit would not only reside in the Messiah and a select few, as in the past, but would be poured out on "all flesh" (Joel 2:28, 29). The Spirit of God was to be the special sign of the age to come and would identify the true Messiah. The people of Israel would be turned into a true messianic people through the life and the power of the Spirit.

The link between Jesus and the Holy Spirit is seen in virtually every aspect of Jesus' life and ministry. His miraculous conception in Mary was by the Holy Spirit (Matthew 1:18, 20; Luke 1:35). Simeon was inspired by the Holy Spirit to bless baby Jesus in the Temple (Luke 2:27, 28). At Jesus' baptism the Spirit came upon Him, confirmed His sonship, and inaugurated His ministry (Matthew 3:16, 17; Mark 1:10, 11; Luke 3:22). Immediately afterward, the Spirit drove Jesus into the wilderness to prepare Him for His ministry (Matthew 4:1; Mark 1:12; Luke 4:1). Following His temptation, Jesus returned to Galilee, full of the Spirit, where His ministry of proclaiming the power and deliverance of the Kingdom commenced in earnest (Luke 4:18, 19).

The power of the Spirit was particularly evident in Jesus' miracles, in the casting out of unclean spirits, and in the forgiveness of sin, which Jesus offered through the Holy Spirit. In Acts 10:38, Luke summarized Jesus' life in these words: "God anointed Jesus of Nazareth with the Holy Spirit and with power, who went about doing good and healing all who were oppressed by the devil, for God was with Him." It was through the eternal Spirit that Jesus offered Himself on the cross (Hebrews 9:14), and through the power of the Spirit He was raised from the dead (Romans 8:11).

One can see more clearly why Jesus commanded His disciples to tarry in Jerusalem and wait for the empowerment of the Holy Spirit before commencing their ministries. They were to be endued with the same presence and power of the Spirit that had motivated and energized the ministry of Jesus (Luke 24:46-49). Jesus personally promised He would send the Holy Spirit upon His disciples for this purpose (Acts 1:8; John 14:16-18). In Acts 2, the promise was fulfilled.

What was the purpose of the continuing work of the Holy Spirit in the lives of Christian believers? To Pentecostals, the message is clear. The power and presence of the Holy Spirit were meant to continue the ministry of Christ in the life of the church. Throughout much of the history of the Christian church, the full manifestation of God's spiritual presence has been hindered and suppressed by truncated theologies and traditions. In these last days, however, God is again pouring out His Spirit as He did in the apostolic era. It is the responsibility of those who receive this gift, Pentecostals believe, to share it with others and to bring to full completion the purpose of Pentecost.

Questions for Reflection

1. If the forefathers of the Church of God could revisit today's church, what aspects of the church's spiritual life do you feel they would be most pleased with? What might disturb them most?

2. What do we mean when we speak of spirituality? Do you feel you could explain it to another person?

3. What exactly do we mean when we speak of the unity of Word and Spirit? Why are both necessary? How do they interrelate?

4. What specific dangers must Pentecostals avoid when they apply a pneumatic hermeneutic to Scripture? Have you witnessed excesses and/or hermeneutical abuses in this regard?

5. Distinguish between the biblical concepts of *chronos* and *kairos*. How does the concept of *kairos* relate to the modern Pentecostal's sense of identity and purpose?

6. Why must Pentecostals always be careful to maintain a Christ-centered approach to spirituality and Christian service?

7. What is the real purpose for the continuing work of the Holy Spirit in the lives of Christian believers today?

Notes

[1]L. Howard Juillerat, *Brief History of the Church of God Evangel* (Cleveland, Tennessee: Church of God Publishing House, 1922), p. 8.

[2]*Ibid.*, p. 9. For a fuller account of the early history of the Church of God, see Charles W. Conn's *Like a Mighty Army*. Conn's work is the official history of the church.

[3]The three evangelists were actually laymen. One was a Methodist (William Martin) and two were Baptists (Joe M. Tipton and Milton McNabb), but all three preached holiness from a Wesleyan perspective. As the spiritually starved listened and responded to their message, a number were filled with the Holy Spirit and spoke in tongues as the Spirit gave the utterance. It should be noted that those who received their Spirit-baptism in this meeting did so 10 years prior to the Azusa Street outpouring in Los Angeles, California (1906), which is popularly regarded as the beginning of the modern Pentecostal Movement.

[4]The annual General Assembly (later it would meet biennially) became a prominent feature of the Church of God. The General Assembly is the highest governing body in the Church of God and is composed of all members who wish to attend and participate in its meetings.

[5]The name "Church of God" was chosen because of its scriptural usage in 1 Corinthians 1:2 and 2 Corinthians 1:1.

[6]For an excellent treatment of our heritage in missions, evangelism, education, and other vital ministries, see Donald N. Bowdle, ed., *The Promise and the Power* (Cleveland, Tenn.: Pathway Press), 1980.

[7]When we speak of spirituality and religious experience, we are in no way trying to accentuate the spectacular. We are not alluding so much to visions, ecstasies,

raptures, or exalted states of consciousness as we are to religious experiences that bring a calm assurance of the reality of one's relationship with God. The natural consequence of such a relationship is joy and a sense of meaning.

[8]In exalting Scripture as the final authority in matters of faith and practice, and in relating the authority of Scripture to experience by the living witness of the Holy Spirit, Pentecostals stand in the tradition of classical Protestantism (Luther and Calvin) and of Wesley.

[9]John Calvin, *Institutes of the Christian Religion.* John Allen, trans. I.ix. 3.

[10]Principally because of their understanding of the relation of Word and Spirit (a view not always theologically articulated), Pentecostals have been able to affirm the verbal inspiration of the Scripture without resorting to the rationalistic, mechanistic, and authoritarian approach to Scriptures that is characteristic of some fundamentalists. On the other hand, this belief has saved them from the excesses of more subjectivistic, existential, and relativistic approaches common to more liberal-minded groups in the modern era.

[11]Louis Dupre and Don Saliers, eds., *Christian Spirituality: Post-Reformation and Modern* (New York: Crossroad, 1989), pp. 490, 491. See also Steven J. Land, *A Passion for the Kingdom: An Analysis and Revision of Pentecostal Spirituality* (Ph.D. dissertation, Emory University, 1990). Land's work has recently been published by Sheffield Academic Press, Sheffield, England.

[12]French L. Arrington, "Hermeneutics, Historical Perspectives on Pentecostals and Charismatics," *Dictionary of Pentecostal and Charismatic Movements* (eds. S.M. Burgess, G.B. McGee, and P.H. Alexander; Grand Rapids: Zondervan, 1988), p. 382.

As Arrington points out, there are potential dangers attached to this approach to Scripture. The first is the ever-present danger of confusing one's own spirit with the Spirit of God, thus claiming an authority for one's own experience that may put it on a par with the authority of Scripture. Another danger is the tendency to avoid the academic preparation that is often necessary in the interpretation and understanding of historical texts. It should be emphasized, however, that these are potential outcomes—not necessary ones.

[13]Paul Tillich, *Systematic Theology*, vol. 3 (Chicago: University of Chicago Press, 1964), pp. 370, 371.

[14]It is essential to maintain a Christocentric criterion for all piety and action. Otherwise, "theologies of experience" may be tempted to qualitatively go beyond the spiritual presence in Jesus. Historical precedents for this include the Montanists, the radical Franciscans, some Anabaptists, and some modern Charismatics.

CHAPTER 2

THE SPIRITUAL
CHARACTER
OF A
PENTECOSTAL
COMMUNITY

Our Pentecostal forefathers believed God was calling them to reclaim the power of Pentecost. God had poured out His Spirit on the church 1,900 years before. What was needed now was for the church to surrender afresh to the sovereign working of the Holy Spirit and reclaim, as individuals and as a community, the apostolic doctrine, fellowship, authentic worship, and compassionate outreach that characterized the Pentecostal community in the Book of Acts.

New Testament Christians were not perfect. They had their problems, their excesses, and an imperfect understanding of what God had in mind for them to be and do. But unmistakable marks of spirituality in the early Christian community characterized the Spirit-filled Christian church. Pentecost had not only changed individuals, but it also changed the character of the church. Consequently, modern Pentecostals yearned to live in the fullness of power that had indwelt the first Christian community.

A Bold and Courageous Faith

An obvious consequence of Pentecost was the supernatural way the experience strengthened the faith of Jesus' disciples, giving them the conviction and boldness they needed to carry on the mission of the church. After the Crucifixion, Jesus' disciples fled into Galilee. Fearful of Romans and Jews, they pondered an uncertain future. Fear had turned them into a band of discouraged fugitives. What they needed most was spiritual courage and boldness. The pouring out of the Spirit at Pentecost gave the church this much-needed power.

The same Peter who had quailed before the pointed finger of a servant and denied his Lord now boldly blamed the Sanhedrin for the murder of the Prince of life (Acts 2:23; 3:13-15; 4:8-10). Peter and John were arrested and arraigned. When the Jewish rulers "saw the boldness of Peter and John, and perceived that they were uneducated and untrained men, they marveled. And they realized that they had been with Jesus" (Acts 4:13). The disciples' demeanor and speech showcased their newfound boldness and courage.

Stephen, the first Christian martyr, was arrested, falsely accused and insulted. But Luke records: "All who sat in the council, looking steadfastly at him, saw his face as the face of an angel" (Acts 6:15). The work of the Holy Spirit in emboldening Christian believers for witness and service in the apostolic church was as significant as His work of convicting and converting sinners. Without this Spirit-inspired boldness and certainty of faith, the New Testament church would have surely failed in its mission.

The same kind of boldness and courage characterized the lives and ministries of the early 20th-century Pentecostal pioneers. Our Pentecostal forefathers made extreme sacrifices for the cause of the gospel they preached. One can read deeply moving accounts of the sacrificing spirit of these pioneers in diaries and biographies that recount their lives and ministries. One reads, for example, of A.J. Tomlinson's sacrificial leadership, of Evangelist J.W. Buckalew's persistence in the face of constant persecution, and of Herman Lauster's imprisonment in a Nazi concentration camp because he refused to stop preaching the gospel. One reads of sacrifice to self and family in men like J.B. Ellis and Paul H. Walker. One reads of undaunted commitment to take the message around the world in missionaries like R.M. Evans, J.H. Ingram, Edmond and Pearl Stark, and Margaret Gaines.

Church of God ministers were ridiculed and persecuted for advocating pacifism during World War I, for trusting in divine healing instead of medicines and physicians, and for following moral standards that stood above the mores of the community. Historian Vinson Synan describes a typical instance of ridicule and persecution that Pentecostal believers in Tennessee had to endure when the movement was young:

> Heavy persecutions broke out against the people. . . . Several houses were burned as mobs led by leading Methodist and Baptist members ransacked and pillaged the homes of the [Pentecostal] worshippers. . . . An important reason for the widespread hostility . . . was the suspicion that everything odd and erroneous was believed and practiced by them. Whenever a Pentecostal meeting took place in a community, rumors were rife about "magic powders," "trances," "wild emotion," and sexual promiscuity. . . . These rumors eventually entered the folklore of the nation and stamped anyone claiming to be "holiness" or "Pentecostal" with the epithet "holy roller." Those who engaged in this "religion of knock-down-and-drag-out" were considered uncultured and uneducated "poor white trash" who inhabited the outer fringes of society. A member of one of the traditional churches who joined a Pentecostal church was generally considered to have "lost his mind" and to have severed his normal social connections.[1]

A radical kind of boldness and conviction was evident as much in the early days of the 20th-century Pentecostal Movement as it was in the apostolic church. The Holy Spirit sustained and encouraged the church at the point of its need. Spiritual boldness and courage have always been distinguishing marks of a true Pentecostal church. In our extremity, when we do not know what we need, the Holy Spirit is present to encourage and renew our will. He comforts in affliction and gives peace and joy during trial and persecution. He intercedes for us according to the will of God (Romans 8:26, 27). Before Jesus ascended to heaven, He promised He would send the Holy Spirit to be a special Comforter and Helper. The Holy Spirit would be the Paraclete—One who would be alongside in time of need. Christians throughout the centuries have confirmed the fact that the Spirit is always near.

Ministering in the Power of the Holy Spirit

The primary mission of Pentecost was to proclaim the gospel. Jesus promised the Holy Spirit to His disciples so they could effectively bear witness to Him (Acts 1:8). To tarry in Jerusalem until they were empowered by the Holy Spirit was necessary before the church could go into all the world and preach the gospel (Luke 24:47-49). Christian missions and Pentecost are inseparably linked. Pentecost was the necessary preparation for missions, and missions was the logical and inevitable result of Pentecost. Jesus accomplished His earthly mission in the power of the Spirit; the church would carry out its mission in that same power. This is the strategy God planned.

The first miracle recorded after the Day of Pentecost was the healing of the lame man at the gate of the Temple. The account of this healing, however, was not merely to tell about a miracle. It was to lead to the question the authorities asked, "By what power or by what name have you done this?"

Peter answered, "By the name of Jesus Christ of Nazareth, whom you crucified, whom God raised from the dead" (Acts 4:7-10).

Miracles were commonplace in Acts. They were more than displays of power, however. They provided opportunities and forums for witness. "With great power the apostles gave witness to the resurrection of the Lord Jesus. And great grace was upon them all" (4:33). "They did not cease," we are told, "teaching and preaching Jesus as the Christ" in the Temple and in their homes (5:42).

The ministry of the apostle Paul fits the same pattern. He proclaimed the gospel with power. He told the Corinthians he preached "in demonstration of the Spirit and of power" (1 Corinthians 2:4). He reminded the Thessalonians the "gospel came to [them] not simply with words, but also with power, with the Holy Spirit and with deep conviction" (1 Thessalonians 1:5, *NIV*). Paul wrote to the Romans that he would "not venture to speak of anything except what Christ has accomplished through me . . . by what I have said and done—by the power of signs and miracles, through the power of the Spirit" (Romans 15:18, 19, *NIV*).

Pentecost not only fulfilled the prophecy of Joel that the Spirit would be poured out "on all flesh" (2:28) but the desire of Moses as well, that "all the Lord's people [would be] prophets" (Numbers 11:29). It also fulfilled Isaiah's expectation that the pouring out of God's Spirit would be followed by a confession of the Lord's name (Isaiah 44:3-5). The influence of the Holy Spirit on the early church was so intense it could not be content until it had taken the gospel "to the end of the earth" (Acts 1:8). When Christians today are filled with the Spirit as the 120 were on the Day of Pentecost, they too will be empowered for the witnessing mission. The character of a Spirit-filled community is to minister and bear witness to its Lord.

Someone said Jesus did not leave the church with a philosophy but with a set of active verbs. Thus, the finest expressions of appreciation for the role of the Holy Spirit in the life of the witnessing church usually comes from those actively involved in evangelism and missions. Those involved in the struggles and triumphs of evangelism and the missionary enterprise have a special appreciation for the Spirit's role in witnessing. Like weapons of war, the value of the Spirit is better assessed on the field of action. Christ did not promise the church His presence and power amid inactivity. Jesus promised to be with the church in the person of the Holy Spirit, as believers "go," "tell," and "make disciples." The work of the Holy Spirit is tied to our action as witnesses. There is no promise of power where there is no witness, for the power of Pentecost exists for that purpose.

When the Pentecostal revival broke out in Kansas, Texas, California, North Carolina, and Tennessee at the beginning of this century, the movement itself became a witness to the evangelistic mission of Pentecost. Evangelism and missions became virtually synonymous with the Pentecostal experience. Since the late '50s the Spirit has penetrated nearly every historic denomination. Anglicans, Catholics, Lutherans, Presbyterians, Baptists, Methodists, Mennonites, Quakers, the Salvation Army, and many other groups have experienced the dynamic moving of the Holy Spirit and have become missionary movements. The Holy Spirit recognizes no boundaries. As He did in the early church, the Holy Spirit has hurdled every social, economic, racial, and national barrier. The explosive growth of the Pentecostal/Charismatic movements in the latter half of the 20th century has been the most significant factor in the unprecedented growth of evangelical Christianity. According to church growth experts, Pentecostals currently comprise the largest family of Protestants in the world.[2]

History confirms what Scripture teaches. The character of the church is always transformed by the living presence of the Holy Spirit. Since the outbreak of the Charismatic Movement, it is common in all religious circles to speak about theological renewal, liturgical renewal, structural renewal, pastoral renewal, and the renewal of the laity. The fact is that whenever and wherever the Holy Spirit is allowed to operate freely, the church will be renewed in all dimensions of its life so that it can truly be a church that witnesses and ministers in power. It was this way in the apostolic church; it is still that way today. It is part of our Pentecostal heritage.

Through a Worshiping Church. The church of the New Testament fulfilled its intended function as a witnessing and worshiping community only after it was reconstituted by the Spirit. The new wine of the Spirit needed new institutional wineskins. Until Pentecost the institutions through which the church worshiped and ministered were based in Judaism. At Pentecost the institutions of Judaism were transformed to accommodate the new reality of the Spirit.[3]

Before Pentecost the Temple was the central place of worship, the priest the central office-bearer, the altar the central object, and the sacrifice the central act of worship. After Christ's coming the Holy Spirit transformed the worship of the church. Jesus' conversation with the woman of Samaria anticipated the coming end of worship at the Temple. "The hour is coming," Jesus said, "when you will neither on this mountain, nor in Jerusalem, worship the Father. . . . True worshipers will worship the Father in spirit and truth; for the Father is seeking such to worship Him. God is Spirit, and those who worship Him must worship in spirit and truth" (John 4:21-24). Jewish worship was confined to the Temple and to tightly regulated forms and rituals. True spiritual worship, Jesus indicated, would soon be different.

Early Christians worshiped in both formal and informal settings. They no longer attended the sacrifices in the Temple, for they knew that these sacrifices had been fulfilled through the sacrifice of Jesus. They did, however, continue to attend the prayer services in the Temple (Acts 3:1). Their break with institutional Judaism was made in a patient and orderly manner. At every opportunity they increasingly met together for fellowship, the breaking of bread, and worship in each other's homes.

Acts 2 describes the form and spirit of early Christian worship: "And they continued steadfastly in the apostles' doctrine and fellowship, in the breaking of bread, and in prayers" (v. 42). "Continuing daily with one accord in the temple, and breaking bread from house to house, they ate their food with gladness and simplicity of heart, praising God, and having favor with all the people. And the Lord added to the church daily those who were being saved" (v. 46).

Through a Learning Church. *It is interesting and significant that the first mark of the Spirit-filled church mentioned in Acts 2:42-47 is study.* The early Christians literally devoted themselves to the apostles' teaching. This was a learning and studying church. "The Holy Spirit had opened a school in Jerusalem," John R.W. Stott notes, "and the apostles were the appointed teachers in the school."

> The new converts were not enjoying some mystical experience that led them to despise their intellect. There was no anti-intellectualism. They did not despise the mind. They did not disdain theology, nor did they suppose that instruction was unnecessary. They did not say that because they had received the Holy Spirit, He was the only teacher they needed and they could dispense with human teachers.
>
> Some people today say that, but these early, Spirit-filled Christians did not. They sat at the apostles' feet, they devoted themselves to the apostles' teaching, they were hungry for apostolic instruction. They were eager to learn all they could. They knew Jesus had authorized the apostles to be the infallible teachers of the church, so they submitted to the apostles' authority.[4]

From a New Testament perspective, learning and education can never be rightly divorced from true spirituality. Christians have no biblical grounds for dichotomizing the heart from the head. God gives us our minds as well as our emotions and our will. We are to love Him with our minds as well as with our heartfelt emotions. Spirit-filled Christians ought always to approach learning and study as an act of worship, humbly bowing the mind before the Author of all truth.

Through a Unified Church. *A second mark of spiritual worship in the apostolic church was their unity in the Spirit, their togetherness and fellowship.* The unity of the early church was more than mere friendship and camaraderie; it was *koinonia.* It was the fellowship of the Holy Spirit—the kind of fellowship that produces a true community of believers. Koinonia gives our "togetherness" a spiritual dimension that can never be duplicated in secular gatherings. Ray Hughes, prominent Church of God minister and administrator, describes the effects koinonia has had in the Church of God:

> This all-pervasive spirit of fraternal affection is one of the fruits of the fullness of the Holy Ghost. The love of God is shed abroad in our hearts by the Holy Ghost. The cordial and warm fellowship of the Church of God has made a distinct and extraordinary impression upon believers. In fact, this exhibition of love and concern for one another has convinced sinners of the love of God. They see a radiation and a reflection of the love of God in the fellowship of believers.

There is no place for isolation in Pentecostal worship. Pentecostal worship provides for fellowship, comforting, edifying, exhorting, and praying for one another. This is the corporate nature of worship, consequently, the necessity for involvement of the total body in the worship service of the church. This is also a strong case for consistent attendance at the house of God. The "fellowship of the saints" provides strength, courage, and edification for the believers.[5]

Those who are open to and desirous of the operation of the Holy Spirit and spiritual gifts in the church are often referred to as "charismatics."[6] Spiritual gifts, or *charismata*, have their origin in the gracious (Greek, *charis*—"grace") operation of the Holy Spirit and are bestowed to equip God's people for worship and service. Worship is the life of the church. Through its worship the church witnesses to the resurrected Lord who lives in the church through the Holy Spirit. For this reason, Pentecostal worship is joyous and alive. It is regularly punctuated with praise, the clapping and uplifting of hands, concert prayer, and occasional times of uninhibited shouting and rejoicing as the people of God respond to the spiritual presence and power of God.

When the church is a living reality convinced of Christian truth in heart and mind, when the church is inspired to worship and equipped to proclaim Christ by the power of the Holy Spirit, it becomes a charismatic community. The structures of the church and its order of worship are meant to reflect both the freedom of the Spirit to operate in the church and the fact that the grace of God ministered through the church is continuous and faithful.[7] When the church hears the Word of God, it is reminded of God's faithfulness to His promises. When it breaks the bread and drinks from the cup, it remembers the continuity of His grace. Pentecostals are widely known for anointed and spirited singing, but singing too must reflect both the freedom of the Spirit and the faithful continuity of God's grace. Paul L. Walker, a prominent Pentecostal pastor, writes about the need for a balanced approach to spiritual singing in the church:

If we fail to sing the traditional hymns, then we are robbing ourselves and our children of the historical heritage of praise to God. If we abandon our unique gospel song, then we are missing the music of the heart which brings a warmth of communion and depth of expression so necessary for the fullness of God's presence. If we fail to utilize the intimacy of the chorus, then we miss the spontaneity of worship which transcends the usual and routine to bring the service into personal relationship with God. We need it all, but let it be chosen in "holy taste" which will be edifying to the church because it glorifies God.[8]

In Pentecostal worship services there is usually a free-flowing operation of the *charismata*, but the need to remember the purpose for spiritual gifts in the church is a real one. The gifts can never be rightly separated from the Giver. Jesus Christ is the Giver of gifts (Ephesians 4:7-13). In giving the Holy Spirit, He gives His church all that is necessary to its life and its mission. The Holy Spirit operates in believers, then, to witness to and glorify Jesus Christ. When Christ is exalted, the church is built up.

The *charismata* are not limited to a special class or rank of Christians. All Christians are graciously gifted for Christian service. The priesthood of all believers should be evident when the church is structured charismatically. The church ought never to organize itself or structure its worship to exclude any of the people of God (the *laos*) from meaningful participation. The *charismata* are not limited to the clergy, administrators, or officeholders. Leadership is necessary in the church, and the Holy Spirit gifts men and women for that function. But He does not bestow gifts on individuals for the purpose of creating a leading class to dominate the body. The mark of spiritual leadership is service (*diakonia*), not domination.

Spiritual gifts should never become objects of pride. When they do, the individual is exalted and division occurs in the body. Every member of the body should exercise the gift(s) given him or her by the Holy Spirit. They are given to build up the whole body of Christ (Romans 12). The completeness of the body depends on the participation of every member. The unity of the body depends on every member's selfless consideration of others. An individual's gift is not a measure for others; rather, the edification of others is the measuring stick for the exercise of an individual's gift.

There is a need and a place for the more extraordinary gifts in the church. But these should not be emphasized at the expense of less conspicuous gifts which are just as important to the proper functioning of the body. An examination of Paul's lists of spiritual gifts reveals the Holy Spirit has varied the gifts in order to serve the total needs of the church. Spiritual gifts are related to such diverse tasks as preaching, giving, teaching, administration, helping, and so forth (1 Corinthians 12:1-12; Romans 12:6-8; Ephesians 4:11). The importance of a spiritual gift lies not in its miraculous quality or unusual manifestation but in its responsible place in the church so that the whole body may be built up and equipped for service (1 Corinthians 12:7).

Spiritual gifts must always be practiced in ways consistent with the clear teachings of Scripture. Virtually every gift has its carnal counterfeit. The only safeguard against error is the truth of the Word. The Word judges everything that lays claim to one's trust and obedience. It is the responsibility of the church to "test the spirits to see whether they are from God" (1 John 4:1, *NIV*). While the church is a pneumatic reality (1 Corinthians 3:16; Ephesians 2:22; 1 Peter 2:5), it is nevertheless a spiritual reality built on the authoritative witness of the prophets and apostles. The church is likened to a spiritual building, a temple for the habitation of God through the Spirit (Ephesians 2:19-22). Jesus Christ himself is the cornerstone of the building. When the church is founded on Him, it is like a house built on a rock that cannot be moved or eroded by floods of evil and error (Luke 6:48).

Institutional Structures

Saying the church is a charismatic community does not suggest that the church has no need for institutional structure. Some who regard themselves as "spiritual" tend to think of the church as a free-floating enterprise, operating within some kind of twilight zone without need for order or structure. Of course this is not the case. As the *Logos* took on human form in Jesus Christ, so the church needs some structural form through which Christ's work can be extended to the world through the power of the Holy Spirit.

Church structures have both practical and symbolic functions. On the practical side they help facilitate the church's mission. The need for organizational structure was evident in the New Testament itself, as the Jerusalem Council (Acts 15) and the Pastoral Epistles attest. It was inevitable that the church as a pilgrim community would organize itself and take on an institutional form as its numbers grew. Organizational structure could indeed serve an instrumental good. But there were (and are) real dangers.

The danger which organization and institutional structures pose for Kingdom life lies not in the structures themselves but in the propensity individuals have to depend on the power of organization and the forms of life it generates. The tendency is for structures to become impersonal, bureaucratic, and competitive. The church can easily shape itself after the model of secular structures, organized for efficiency and profit. When it does, however, the people of God tend to be valued primarily for their loyalty to the organization. Leaders become managers following principles of modern management rather than leading by spiritual example.

This is not the kind of life in the body that Christ intended. His purpose was to form a community of loving, caring, serving believers. The so-called "spiritual church" and "organized church" will always need each other. They cannot be separated, but neither should they be confused. The former provides the agenda, the vision, and inspiration. The latter provides the vehicle through which the purpose and ideal of the spiritual church finds expression. The organized church must be constantly renewed. Only as it finds renewal through the living Christ can it maintain its vision and fulfill its purpose. When the institutional church loses contact with its spiritual center, it loses meaning and purpose.

Church structures are necessary too because they symbolize and reflect the faithfulness of God. This symbol is essential to our understanding of God. Order and organization bespeaks the continuity of God's grace and His faithfulness to His people. God's steadfastness remains when all else in the world seems chaotic and uncertain. The assembled church is reminded over and over of God's steadfast love through the order and structure of the church. Like creeds and declarations of faith, church structure gives shape to one's faith.

R.P. Johnson, early Church of God pioneer and spiritual leader, spoke of the necessary compatibility of government and spirituality:

> Two outstanding essentials in the Church of God, as revealed by the New Testament, are spirituality and government. For a people to attempt to establish a church without spirituality would be like having an empty form—a corpse. And without government, a church would be indiscernible, having neither office nor officer, rule nor ruler, ordinance nor order. There would be no authority in any wise to attend to church business. We confidently expect to see the Church of God maintain the Bible standard of doctrine and victory—thereby being kept from apostasy—because our organization recognizes and appreciates the necessity and blessedness of both. [9]

Love and Service

Above everything else a truly Pentecostal community is a Christian community. This means a loving and serving community. The purpose of the Holy Spirit is not to close believers up in themselves but to open them up toward others in self-giving (*agape*) love. True spirituality is characterized by an outward as well as an inward and upward orientation.

Jesus taught that the whole Law is contained in love of God and neighbor (Matthew 22:34-40). Love is the distinguishing mark of Christian discipleship (John 13:34, 35). God's love has been poured into our hearts through the Holy Spirit (Romans 5:5), and this love is the Christian's ethical norm and way of life (Galatians 5:6). It is, Paul declared, "the most excellent way" (1 Corinthians 12:31, *NIV*). Love is the greatest of God's spiritual gifts. Without it, other spiritual gifts profit nothing:

> If I speak in the tongues of men and of angels, but have not love, I am only a resounding gong or a clanging cymbal. . . . If I have a faith that can move mountains, but have not love, I am nothing. If I give all I possess to the poor and surrender my body to the flames, but have not love, I gain nothing (1 Corinthians 13:1-3, *NIV*).

Love should not be confused with emotion or sentimentality. The kind of love Jesus, Paul, and John alluded to is the kind of love that manifests itself in self-giving action. Love feeds the hungry, clothes the naked, befriends the friendless, sets captives free. It is not enough for the church to function merely as a referral agency. It is not enough to turn people over to God with a pious "God bless you" without the benefit of our Spirit-inspired acceptance and concern. Love must be enfleshed in us and in our actions just as it was in Jesus.

A little girl kept calling her father to her room during a violent thunderstorm. After several visits the father tried to comfort his daughter by telling her she had nothing to fear, that God was there and He would take care of everything. "Yes, Daddy, I know God is here," the little girl replied, "but right now I need somebody with skin on." The world desperately needs to see a Jesus with skin on, One who has been enfleshed in believers through the power of the Holy Spirit.

Some tend to polarize "social activism" and "evangelicalism," artificially separating those who would save souls from those who would feed the hungry, minister to derelicts and outcasts, and liberate the oppressed. But this kind of dichotomy only reveals an ignorance of the Word and the mission of Jesus. One would advocate a half-Jesus of evangelism without social action, the other a half-Jesus of social activism without evangelism. Isolated, both ultimately fall because neither focuses clearly on the true mission of Jesus or the character of the church. When the mission of Jesus shapes our own and the Holy Spirit is allowed to inspire our love and action, one cannot exist without the other. The church cannot bear true witness to Jesus Christ in a way that is faithful to itself without becoming involved in human need and suffering.

Jesus saw people as whole persons. He did not separate physical needs from spiritual needs. Jesus offered wholeness of body, mind, and spirit, as well as holiness of heart. When Christians see people only in terms of spirits and souls, they see less than Jesus saw, and they will inevitable offer less than Jesus offered. If we are to minister as Jesus ministered, we must not allow the holy Spirit to be removed from the physical and social realities of life, neither in our thinking nor in our actions.

Susana Vaccaro de Petrella, a Pentecostal leader in Argentina, puts the matter in a perspective that all Pentecostals can appreciate:

> We believe there are two elements that are indispensable to any Christian community: spiritual renewal and commitment to freedom, justice and peace. If we limit ourselves to the first, we reduce the gospel to an otherworldly state of glory. If we limit ourselves to the second, we fall inevitably into the error of attempting to do good for its own sake. But our Spirit-inspired Pentecostal message is charged with the strong desire both for spiritual renewal and for the liberation that every human being needs so as to live in a climate of freedom, justice and peace.[10]

The apostolic church exemplified this perspective. Love and concern for the poor in their midst prompted early Christians to voluntarily sell their possessions and share all things with those in need (Acts 2:44, 45). They were not trying to control the forces of history or police the ethics of the world. They were simply trying to bear witness to the kingdom of God and the righteousness that characterizes that Kingdom. As Stanley Hauerwas has noted, "The first social ethical task of the church is to be the church—the servant community. The church does not have a social ethic; the church is a social ethic."[11]

Concern for those in need and those who suffer was never meant to be something tacked on to the gospel for good measure, to round it all out. A genuine concern for the welfare of others is part of the gospel itself. It is the surest proof we have of the gospel's power to penetrate and transform our lives. The only terms under which the world can be truly liberated are Christ's terms. It is the church's responsibility to express through word and deed the liberation it already knows in Jesus Christ.

Social concern is a vital part of the Pentecostal heritage. Through its care for the sick, the poor, the orphaned, unwed mothers, drug addicts and alcoholics, runaways, the lonely, and those dispossessed by misfortune or natural disasters, the church continues to bear witness to its love and its service.[12]

An Inclusive Community

The story of 20th-century Pentecost serves to remind us that Christianity is a catholic faith. This means it is a faith for the entire human family as well as a faith for the whole person. Its universality is seen in its inclusion of all in the community of faith who are willing to come under the lordship of Jesus Christ. Jesus demonstrated a special concern for the despised, the outcasts, and those discriminated against by society: lepers, tax collectors, Samaritans, women, children, the poor. His gospel was so elevating and transforming that Paul could write, "There is neither Jew nor Greek . . . slave nor free . . . male nor female; for you are all one in Christ Jesus" (Galatians 3:28). This would have been inconceivable to a Jew a generation before. Unlike those who used the law to bind and oppress, Jesus challenged every interpretation of the law that made it an instrument of human bondage and oppression.

When an imprisoned and discouraged John the Baptist sent a messenger to Jesus asking if He was really the Christ, or should John look for another, Jesus responded, "The blind receive their sight and the lame walk; the lepers are cleansed and the deaf hear; the dead are raised up and the poor have the gospel preached to them" (Matthew 11:5). Jesus was not only doing the expected works of the Messiah, He was doing them for the benefit of the rejected castaways of His society. He was ministering to every segment of the population as well as to every aspect of the human person. Through word and deed Jesus revealed that God frees us from the idols of this world—nation, race, wealth, power—that we may love and serve one another. The religion of Jesus was not one of exclusion but of inclusion.

Pentecost continued and accelerated this spirit of inclusiveness. The penetration of the Holy Spirit into the apostolic church knew no social, economic, racial, or national barriers. The Jews had long-standing prejudices against Samaritans in particular and Gentiles in general. But the work of the Spirit in the church after Pentecost served to break down both of these barriers. The martyrdom of Stephen fanned the flames of the church in all directions, and Philip the evangelist was sent by the Holy Spirit to Samaria (Acts 8). Many were saved and baptized. Later, when the apostles laid hands on them, they received the gift of the Holy Spirit. A similar thing happened to Cornelius and his household (Acts 10). While Peter was preaching, the Holy Spirit fell on the whole household of Cornelius. The Jewish Christians with Peter were astonished because "the gift of the Holy Spirit had been poured out on the Gentiles also" (v. 45). From that point the Jewish Christians realized that since the Gentiles had received the identical gift from heaven they had received, God shows no partiality. The Spirit truly was being poured out on "all flesh" in accordance with Joel's prophecy (2:28).

Pentecostals in this century believe they too are a part of the fulfillment of Joel's prophecy. In an atmosphere of spiritual worship where there was true *koinonia* and the Holy Spirit was being poured out, no social distinctions of any kind were ever drawn between rich and poor, male and female, white and black, or other artificial divisions. In the early years of the movement, most members of the Church of God were poor, uneducated, and rural. But Pentecostals were people-oriented and inclusive. Women, children, and every racial and ethnic group had a voice. Synan describes the interracial character of the meetings at Azusa Street, site of one of the original beginnings of the modern Pentecostal Movement:

> As the meetings continued week after week, more and more people began to attend, until by the summer of 1906, people of every race and nationality in the Los Angeles area were mingling in the crowds that pressed into the mission from the street. There was no racial prejudice in the services. Negroes, whites, Chinese and even Jews attended side by side to hear Seymour (a black preacher) preach.

Eventually what began as a local revival in a Negro church became of interest to people all over the nation, regardless of race. In a short while the majority of the attendants were white, but always there was complete integration of the races in the services, one man exclaiming, "The color line was washed away in the blood."[13]

As the Pentecostal Movement spread around the world, it identified with the poor and disinherited and became known as a church that welcomed and reached out to those on the fringes of society. In Latin America, Africa, Indonesia, and Third World countries around the world, Pentecostal churches enjoyed phenomenal growth because they identified with the people and worked among the poor. Pentecostal churches are today enjoying the fruits of that labor.

Questions For Reflection

1. Cite an example of a parallel between the trials and persecution of Christians in the New Testament and those of our Pentecostal pioneers. In what ways does the Holy Spirit help us cope with persecution and suffering?

2. How are Pentecost and the Great Commission inseparably linked? How did Pentecost help fulfill the great Commission? What does it mean to minister in the power of the Holy Spirit?

3. Describe the worship style and worship patterns of the early church. What comparisons/contrasts can you draw between worship in the first-century church and contemporary Pentecostal/Charismatic worship?

4. Does the church need organization and structure? Why? What purpose do they serve?

5. What does it mean to be a loving and serving church? Give specific examples.

6. Is social concern and involvement really a part of a Pentecostal church's responsibility? Why? How should the church fulfill its social obligations?

7. How were racial, national, and gender barriers broken down in the early church? Do you feel the Pentecostal church today is truly an inclusive church?

Notes

[1]Vinson Synan, *The Holiness-Pentecostal Movement in the United States* (Grand Rapids: Eerdmans Publishing Co., 1971), p. 186.

[2]Peter Wagner, "Church Growth," *Dictionary of Pentecostal and Charismatic Movements*, eds. S.M. Burgess, G.B. McGee, and P.H. Alexander (Grand Rapids: Zondervan, 1988), p. 181.

[3]For a thought-provoking treatment of the manner in which the Holy Spirit reconstituted the church in accordance with its new situation, see Henry Boer's *Pentecost and Missions* (Grand Rapids: Eerdmans, 1961).

[4]John R.W. Stott, "Setting the Spirit Free," *Christianity Today*, June 12, 1981, p. 18.

[5]Ray H. Hughes, *Church of God Distinctives* (Cleveland, Tenn.: Pathway Press, 1968), pp. 76, 77.

[6]The term *charismatic* is also commonly used in reference to the Charismatic or neo-Pentecostal Movement. In this sense it refers to the phenomenon of Pentecostal experience within historic churches. There are, however, some significant differences between Charismatic and traditional Pentecostal bodies such as the Church of God, Assemblies of God, Pentecostal-Holiness Church, Foursquare Gospel Church, and the Church of God in Christ. For an analysis of the Charismatic Movement, see P. D. Hocken, "Charismatic Movement," *Dictionary of Pentecostal and Charismatic Movements*, eds. S.M. Burgess, G.B. McGee, and P.H. Alexander (Grand Rapids: Zondervan, 1988), pp. 130-160.

[7]For an excellent treatment of this theme, see Eduard Schweizer's *Church Order in the New Testament*.

[8]Paul L. Walker, *The Ministry of Church and Pastor* (Cleveland, Tenn.: Pathway Press, 1965), p. 54; cited by Hughes, *Church of God Distinctives*, p. 83.

[9]R.P. Johnson, "The Church of God: Two Essentials," *Church of God Evangel*, October 30, 1967, p. 12; cited by Hughes, *Church of God Distinctives*, p. 112.

[10]L.S. Vaccaro de Petrella, "The Tension Between Evangelism and Social Action in the Pentecostal Movement," *International Review of Missions 75*, January 1986, p. 36; cited by Cheryl Bridges Johns, *Pentecostal Formation* (Sheffield, England: Sheffield Academic Press, 1993), p. 96.

[11]Stanley Hauerwas, *The Peaceable Kingdom* (Notre Dame: University of Notre Dame Press, 1983), p. 99. Another of Hauerwas' titles that Pentecostal readers would be interested in is *Resident Aliens* which wrestles with the question of what it means to be a Christian in our time.

[12]In recent years the Church of God has developed and implemented a number of ministries that focus on physical and social as well as spiritual needs. One thinks immediately of the church's Ministry to the Military, its medical missions, prison ministries, and Men and Women of Action (which offers building and construction assistance to the homeless and those displaced by natural disasters). The church also sponsors the Peniel Ministry (drug rehabilitation) in Harrisburg, Pennsylvania; Jireh House (for unmarried mothers) in Portland, Oregon; and the Raymond E. Crowley Center (for abused children) in Sevierville, Tennessee.

[13]Synan, p. 109.

A FULL - GOSPEL HERITAGE

David C. Steinmetz, a church historian, wrote an article for *Theology Today*. In it he talked about the necessity of remembering our past:

People who have lost their memories no longer remember who they are. That means that they can no longer function effectively in the present and that they have no secure plans for the future. They have lost their past, and that has emptied their present of meaning and clouded their future.

We must have contact with the past, if only for the sake of the present and the future.

The church could, I suppose, lose its memory as well. It is certainly tempted to do that often enough, but a church which has lost its memory of the past can only wander aimlessly in the present and despair of its future. The church needs the past, if only for the sake of the present and the future.

The invitation to study the history of the church is not an irrelevant call to forsake the mission of the church and lose oneself in a past no longer recoverable. It is rather a call to abandon peripheral matters, to put an end to aimless meandering and nervous activism, to learn again who we are and to whom we belong. Only when we have regained our identity from the past can we undertake our mission in the present.[1]

Those receiving the Pentecostal blessing and identifying with the Pentecostal movement at the turn of the century regarded the outpouring of the Holy Spirit as a sacred (*kairos*) event as well as a historical (*chronos*) event. They earnestly believed they were part of a special spiritual breakthrough—a *kairos*—ordained by God for an end-time purpose. But participation in a *kairos* event does not mean one does not have a *chronos* (or historical) heritage as well. Sacred events and movements are not historyless. They do not simply fall from the sky or burst from a historical vacuum; they take place in social and historical circumstances where patterns can be discerned, historical connections drawn, and traditions identified and celebrated.

Turn-of-the-century Pentecostal pioneers claimed the power of Pentecost as their spiritual birthright and sought to emulate the spiritual character of the New Testament church. Like all religious movements, however, the Pentecostal Movement had its own historical existence. It was subject to the social, cultural and doctrinal influences that gave it birth and nourishment. In recent years Pentecostals and non-Pentecostals alike have shown interest in the origin and history of the Pentecostal Movement and have made significant discoveries. These discoveries have disabused the notion that the movement suddenly emerged in the mountains of North Carolina and Tennessee, in a small Bible college near Topeka, Kansas, or in a black mission on Azusa Street in Los Angeles. The fact is that the movement did not appear out of nowhere. Nor can it be accounted for in terms of a single spiritual experience, such as the baptism in the Holy Spirit with the evidence of speaking in other tongues.

When the outpourings of the Spirit occurred at the turn of the 20th century and the Pentecostal Movement began, there were indeed aspects of belief and practice that were unique to Pentecostals. But a body of doctrines and practices bequeathed to the movement from 19th-century Wesleyan-Holiness traditions constituted their core beliefs. While Pentecostals would eventually discover their indebtedness to a broad range of influence in the Christian tradition, their full-gospel heritage was directly traceable to the Holiness influences of the 19th century.[2]

The purpose of this chapter is to identify and describe briefly those doctrines and practices. We begin by highlighting the Wesleyan-Arminian understanding of conversion and how it differs from the mainstream reformers, Martin Luther and John Calvin. Then we focus on the Wesleyan-Holiness doctrines of sanctification, divine healing, and the premillennial second coming of Christ.

Doctrine of Salvation

During the medieval centuries the Roman Catholic Church developed an elaborate system of sacraments that embodied their essential understanding and practice of salvation. In *The Four Books of Sentences*, Peter Lombard identified seven sacraments, which the church officially sanctioned at the Council of Florence in 1439. The church at that time understood a sacrament to be a "sacred sign" serving as an instrument of God's grace. The Roman Church taught that through these seven sacraments, one receives grace necessary for salvation and the Christian life. The seven sacraments were baptism, confirmation, the Eucharist (or the Mass), penance, extreme unction, holy orders, and marriage. Since the sacraments were mediated through the institutional church, it was generally believed that the church had the power to dispense or withhold the grace of God.

In the 16th century, Protestant reformers called the sacramental system of the Roman Church into question. Since a sacrament had to be of divine appointment and instituted by Christ, they rejected all but two as sacraments—water baptism and the Lord's Supper. Luther, in his reflections on the sacraments, was particularly troubled by the Roman Church's views on penance, which consisted of contrition, confession, absolution, and satisfaction. Luther found the last two aspects of penance—absolution and satisfaction—most disturbing. The absolution pronounced by the priest was supposedly a conveyance of grace, a remission of sin and eternal punishment, and a removal of guilt. But satisfaction still remained to be rendered, either in this life or in purgatory. Until the penitent rendered satisfaction, he or she could not enter heaven. One usually rendered satisfaction through prayer, fasting, almsgiving, or some other good work. Thus, in the Catholic view, it was necessary to add something to the grace of God by works of satisfaction.

As Luther studied the Scriptures, particularly Romans and Galatians, he found Paul's gospel of grace completely contrary to the Roman Church's understanding of the sacrament of penance. Paul's message centered in the fact that the sinner is justified by grace alone, through faith. Human works add nothing to the grace of God. What troubled Luther as well was how psychologically abusive this doctrine could be. He himself had struggled for years with the notion that he could somehow please God and stand in right relationship to Him *if* he worked hard enough. The end result of all his striving had been total frustration. His despair with righteousness by works as a means of justification drove Luther to the Scriptures and to Paul's theology of grace.

Total Depravity. The whole matter came to a head in 1517, when the church launched a fund-raiser to rebuild Saint Peter's basilica in Rome. The church authorized an ecclesiastic named Tetzel to sell indulgences in Germany. The sale of indulgences was based on the theory that the church could remit penance and punishment in purgatory by drawing on a so-called treasury of merit. The treasury of merit was supposedly a surplus of good works accumulated by Christ, Mary, and other saints. For a freewill contribution to the cause, Tetzel promised a draft, as it were, on this heavenly treasure. This doctrine of indulgences, together with the Catholic concept of works righteousness, drove Luther to challenge the whole tenor and substance of Roman Catholic theology.

What began on October 31, 1517, with Luther's Ninety-five Theses did not end until the Roman Church had been shaken to its foundations. The major theme of Luther's cry for reform was justification by grace alone, through faith. This doctrine, more than any other, represented the heart of Luther's reform.

John Calvin, the great reformer in France and Switzerland, had a different theological emphasis, but his burden was essentially the same—to defend the doctrine of salvation on the grounds of grace alone. Calvin's theology flowed out of his understanding of the majesty and sovereignty of God. This led him to a strong doctrine of predestination. The logic of Scripture, for Calvin, was that God graciously saves whom He wills on the basis of eternal election. This gracious election can never be earned by any amount of good works, not even by good intentions.

Like Luther, Calvin believed in total depravity. In the opening sentence of the *Institutes*, Calvin wrote: "True and substantial wisdom principally consists of two parts, the knowledge of God and the knowledge of ourselves."[3] An essential thing to know about ourselves, Calvin stressed, is that we are depraved creatures. One is a sinner because of sinful transgressions and because of a depraved human nature that continually chooses self instead of God. Every act of sin is a reflection of this sinful state. The only righteousness one can properly claim as a basis for a right relationship with God is the righteousness of Christ. We can in no way point to any merits of our own. Salvation is pure gift. The elect can only passively receive the free gift of salvation that God offers in Jesus Christ. While searching the Scriptures in the fall of 1514, Luther discovered what the righteousness of God means. He wrote:

> There I began to understand that the righteousness of God is that by which the righteous lives by a gift of God, namely by faith. And this is the meaning: the righteousness of God is revealed by the gospel, namely, the passive righteousness with which merciful God justifies us by faith, as it is written, "He who through faith is righteous shall live." Here I felt that I was altogether born again and had entered paradise itself through open gates.[4]

Justification Through Faith. In contrast to a Catholic theology that stressed grace and good works, Luther discovered from Paul that one can stand in right relationship to God only on the basis of God's gracious activity in Jesus Christ. In Christ the believer experiences both forgiveness and power. He is freed from all works which enslave him, but he is bound by the law of love that empowers him to serve his neighbor. In *A Treatise on Christian Liberty*, Luther describes the life of the Christian:

> From faith flows love and joy in the Lord, and from love a joyful, willing and free mind that serves one's neighbor willingly and takes no account of gratitude or ingratitude, of praise or blame, of gain or loss.

For a man does not serve that he may put men
under obligations, he does not distinguish between
friends and enemies, nor does he anticipate their
thankfulness or unthankfulness; but most freely and
willingly he spends himself and all that he has,
whether he wastes all on the thankless or whether
he gains a reward. . . . As our heavenly Father has in
Christ freely come to our help, we also ought freely
to help our neighbor through our body and its
works, and each should become as it were a Christ
to the other, that we may be christs to one another
and Christ may be the same in all; that is, that we
may be truly Christians.[5]

Without the recovery of the vital doctrines of total
depravity and justification through faith alone, it
would have been impossible for the church to recover a sound biblical doctrine of salvation. It is important to note, however, that there were aspects of
Luther's and Calvin's understanding of salvation
that Pentecostals in the Wesleyan-Arminian tradition
would see in a different light.

John Wesley and his followers fully agreed with
Luther and Calvin that we are all depraved creatures. Unaided by divine grace, we can of our own
choice or merit do nothing to bring ourselves back
into right relationship with God. In our depraved
condition we do not even desire such a relationship.
Our will, Luther noted, is bound by the power of sin
that rules our life.[6]

Wesley and those in the Arminian tradition had no
argument with human depravity. Their disagreement with the reformers was not over the issue of
sin but in their different perspectives on the opera-

tion of divine grace. Arminianism drew its under-standing of divine sovereignty and human freedom from Jacob Arminius (1560-1609). This Dutch Reformed theologian's reactions to the deterministic logic of Calvinism gave rise to an anti-Calvinistic movement during the 17th century. John Wesley was influenced by Arminianism and became its best-known advocate in the 18th century. The Arminians sought to reconcile divine sovereignty with real free will in terms of election contingent on God's fore-knowledge of our free choice. While Calvin ground-ed God's saving work in the logic of divine decrees and eternal predestination, Wesley placed his emphasis on faith in Christ and the Atonement. Christ did not die for an elect group of people but for all who believe and put their trust in His saving work. All who respond in faith to Christ will be saved; all who resist or turn away from His grace will be lost.

Prevenient Grace. Wesley's understanding of the work of salvation began with prevenient grace. Prevenient grace is not to be confused with saving grace. It is the grace God gives in preparation for salvation, through the conviction of sin and the drawing of the sinner by the Holy Spirit. Because the sinner is in bondage to sin, God must take the initiative in salvation. Through prevenient grace God restores to the sinner the ability to make a favorable response to God. In freeing the will from its bondage to sin, God is, in effect, giving the sinner the ability to submit to and cooperate with grace that leads to salvation. The fact that God does free the will so it can turn to Him is implied throughout the Scriptures. He exhorts sinners to turn to God, repent, and believe.

The working of this preparatory grace does not mean that all who receive it will necessarily make a permanent decision in the direction of God. It means only that those who receive this grace are capable of acting contrary to their fallen nature. The Scriptures are clear that God wills to save from sin, its power, and its consequences. God does not will to save individuals contrary to their will, however. It is indeed possible to resist the saving grace of God or to turn away from it, though those who do so condemn themselves. Where the Calvinist holds that God offers salvation only on the basis of His sovereign decrees, the Arminian believes that God, through one means or another, extends His prevenient grace to all and that all who respond favorably to this grace can be saved.[7]

Our moral freedom does not impinge on the sovereignty of God, for the exercise of free choice is precisely what a sovereign God has willed. The biblical doctrine of salvation does not negate divine sovereignty or human responsibility. God must initiate the process of salvation, and it is only on the basis of His sovereign grace and mercy that one could ever be saved. It is not our merits nor even our choice that saves, but God's gracious acceptance of us in Jesus Christ. On the other hand, God never imposes His grace on anyone. We must freely choose to cooperate with His prevenient grace if we expect God to bestow the gift of saving faith and repentance.

Just as God foreknew—from the foundations of the world—how Adam and Eve would respond to His command, so He knows how each of us will respond to His prevenient grace. In this sense, one can talk about predestination in a manner that is biblically sound. It is an election based on God's fore-knowledge of our choice (Romans 8:29; 1 Peter 1:1, 2). God's foreknowledge of our choice is not causative—it does not cause our choice any more than God's foreknowledge of Adam's and Eve's choice determined their disobedience. But those whom God foresees will respond favorably to His grace, He determines to save.

On the basis, then, of God's gracious gift of repentance and faith, God justifies the sinner (Galatians 3:11). He regenerates (John 3:3, 5). He sanctifies (Acts 26:18). He keeps those who maintain faith in Christ (1 Peter 1:5).

Justification and Regeneration

Faith in Christ is more than mere assent to God's gracious act of forgiveness. It involves a willingness to allow God to transform one's life. A personal relationship with Christ must, of necessity, bring transformation of life. In justification one is forgiven and accepted by God as a son or daughter, but Wesley emphasized that God wills to do more. God's purpose in salvation is to heal and restore the image of God corrupted through the Fall. Restoring God's image, Wesley believed, involves more than a single operation of God's grace. No distinction exists in time between justification and regeneration. They do, however, represent different moments of grace in the order of salvation. In a sermon Wesley explained the distinction:

> Though it be allowed, that justification and the new birth are, in point of time, inseparable from each other, yet they are easily distinguished, as being not

the same, but things of a widely different nature. Justification implies only a relative, the new birth a real, change. God in justifying us does something for us; in begetting us again, He does the work in us. The former changes our outward relation to God, so that instead of enemies we become children; by the latter our inmost souls are changed, so that instead of sinners we become saints. The one restores us to the favor, the other to the image, of God. The one is the taking away the guilt, the other the taking away the power, of sin: so that, although they are joined together in point of time, yet are they of wholly distinct natures.[8]

Conversion brings a conscious change in the believer. Through the witness of the Spirit the converted believer experiences assurance that he or she is now a child of God (Romans 8:16). In his journal Wesley described how, on May 24, 1738, he experienced assurance of salvation:

> In the evening I went very unwillingly to a society in Aldersgate Street, where one was reading Luther's preface to the *Epistle to the Romans*. About a quarter before nine, while he was describing the change which God works in the heart through faith in Christ, I felt my heart strangely warmed. I felt I did trust in Christ, Christ alone for my salvation; and an assurance was given me that He had taken away my sins, even mine, and saved me from the law of sin and death.[9]

Justification is just the beginning, Wesley believed, of a process whereby the believer grows into the likeness of Christ. All that happens in justification (forgiveness and right standing with God) and the new birth (a changed nature) anticipate the full restoration of God's image in the life of the Christian through a second definite work of divine grace. Wesley described this as entire sanctification, holiness, Christian perfection, perfect love, and full salvation. In his sermons Wesley carefully distinguished between these two operations of divine grace:

> By justification we are saved from the guilt of sin, and restored to the favor of God; by sanctification we are saved from the power and root of sin, and restored to the image of God. All experience, as well as Scripture, show this salvation to be both instantaneous and gradual. It begins in the moment we are justified in the holy, humble, gentle, patient love of God on man. It gradually increases from that moment, as a "grain of mustard-seed, which, at first, is the least of all seeds," but afterwards puts forth large branches, and becomes a great tree; till, in another instant, the heart is cleansed from all sin, and filled with pure love to God and man. But even that love increases more and more, till we "grow up in all things into Him that is our Head"; till we attain "the measure of the stature of the fullness of Christ."[10]

Entire Sanctification

Wesley's doctrine of entire sanctification—or Christian perfection, as it was commonly called—was his great contribution to Methodism and, through Methodism and the Holiness Movement of the 19th century, to the Christian tradition. Luther and Calvin, the great Protestant reformers, recovered and gave to the church a renewed emphasis on the authority of Scripture, justification by faith, and the priesthood of all believers. It remained for Wesley and his holiness followers to recover the biblical doctrine of sanctification and holiness.

Wesley had no intention of promoting sinless living by understating the powerful and subtle effects of original sin. He understood as thoroughly as the reformers the dreadful effect sin has on every human life. Wesley also believed that a pessimism about sin and its effects must be balanced with an optimism about the power of God's grace to deal with the sin problem.[11] Unlike the Catholic view of holiness based on human merit, with purgatory to complete the process, Wesley viewed sanctification as a free gift of grace found through a living and unbroken relationship with Jesus Christ. Holiness is possible not through acts of merit or through acts of separation from sin but through the cleansing blood of Christ. A commitment to Jesus Christ is indeed a commitment to separate oneself unto God and to God's holy purpose for one's life. Similarly, one must be willing to separate oneself from sin. But acts of separation without a consecrated fellowship with Christ will only become a form of self-righteous pharisaism.

Holiness, Wesley emphasized, can only be found in Jesus Christ and one's daily relationship with Him. No one is perfect in keeping the demands of the moral law. In the light of these demands, we stand condemned before God. But in Jesus Christ we can stand before God perfected by the merits of our Savior. Colin Williams, a Wesley scholar, notes that the perfection Wesley taught has to do with one's relationship to Christ and not to the moral law.

This relationship, made possible through the work of the Holy Spirit, fills one with love for God and neighbor daily. It is not a perfection from ignorance or error but a perfection of motive and desire. It is, in a word, a perfection in love. In his writings Wesley explained what he meant by Christian perfection:

> But whom then do you mean by "one that is perfect"? We mean one in whom is "the mind which was in Christ," and who so "walketh as Christ also walked"; a man "that hath clean hands and a pure heart," or that is "cleansed from all filthiness of flesh and spirit"; one in whom is "no occasion of stumbling," and who accordingly "does not commit sin. . . ." We understand hereby, one whom God hath "sanctified throughout in body, soul, and spirit. . . ."
>
> This man can now testify to all mankind, "I am crucified with Christ: nevertheless I live; yet not I, but Christ liveth in me. . . ." He "loveth the Lord his God with all his heart," and serveth Him "with all his strength." He "loveth his neighbor," every man, "as himself"; yea, "as Christ loveth us. . . ." Indeed his soul is all love, filled with "bowels of mercies, kindness, meekness, gentleness, longsuffering." And his life agreeth thereto, full of "the work of faith, the patience of hope, the labor of love. . . ."
>
> This is to be a perfect man, to be "sanctified throughout"; even "to have a heart so all-flaming with the love of God," "as continually to offer up every thought, word, and work, as a spiritual sacrifice, acceptable to God through Christ."[12]

When does this perfection in love take place in the life of the Christian believer? Wesley's answer to this question was twofold: he believed it is both a gradual and an instantaneous work of grace. The gradual nature of God's sanctifying grace both precedes and follows the instantaneous work. In the believer's day-to-day relationship with Christ, a gradual transformation takes place in preparation for the gift. After the instantaneous work has occurred, the need for sanctifying grace continues so that those who have been "perfected" in love may continue to grow and flourish. But there comes a time when an instantaneous change occurs and the old Adamic nature is purged from the believer's life. A "perfection of unbroken conscious dependence upon Christ" begins.[13] The fact that many have no conscious awareness of this work in no way negates the fact that it occurs. As Wesley noted:

> It is often difficult to perceive the instant when a man dies; yet there is an instant in which life ceases. And if even sin ceases, there must be a last moment of its existence, and a first moment of our deliverance from it.[14]

Those who do not expect and receive it earlier must receive it just prior to death, for the Scriptures teach that apart from holiness no one will see the Lord (Hebrews 12:14). Christians have no right to seek a life of "cheap grace" but are to actively wait for the sanctifying experience. To the question of how one is to wait for this change, Wesley replied:

> Not in careless indifference, or indolent inactivity; but in vigorous, universal obedience, in a zealous keeping of all the commandments, in watchfulness and painfulness, in denying ourselves, and taking up our cross daily; as well as in earnest prayer and fasting, and a close attendance on all the ordinances

of God. And if any man dream of attaining it in any other way, (yea, or of keeping it when it is attained, when he has received it even in the largest measure), he deceiveth his own soul. It is true, we receive it by simple faith; but God does not, will not, give that faith, unless we seek it with all diligence, in the way which he hath ordained.[15]

Rise of the Holiness Movement

Wesley's theology of a second, perfecting work of divine grace became the distinguishing doctrine of Methodism. The Methodist church was the first great Holiness church, and its beliefs and practices were soon being transplanted to America through outstanding preachers and organizers like Francis Asbury and Richard Wright. Methodism soon became the fastest-growing religious movement on the American frontier. It appealed to the common people because of its emotional presentation, its warmth, its emphasis on experience, and its appeal to morality. Methodism was, as Wesley described it, a "religion of the heart." For those grown weary of creeds, permissiveness, and the formal worship of the times, Methodism offered an almost irresistible alternative. By the turn of the 19th century, Methodist circuit riders had spread the holiness message throughout the frontier, and the "second blessing" was being preached in camp meetings like the famous Cane Ridge meeting in Logan County, Kentucky (1800).

Camp meetings became a regular part of American religious life, as the holiness message was preached with zeal and emotion. By 1836 Charles

Finney was preaching sanctification in the old revival districts of western New York. In 1837 he joined Asa Mahan at Oberlin College, where the message was given academic respectability through the so-called Oberlin theology. John Humphrey Noyes preached the sanctification doctrine at Yale until he was asked to leave. Phoebe Palmer and her physician husband preached sanctification throughout Canada and the United States. In England, William E. Boardman interpreted the holiness message to those outside the Wesleyan tradition and influenced the Keswick movement. British periodicals and church papers were soon extolling the message of sanctification and the victorious "higher life" that Christians could enjoy.

By mid-century this country was drifting toward political division and Civil War. The message of holiness began to wane as more and more attention was focused on the politics of slavery. War soon diminished hope for the personal and social perfection heralded by holiness advocates. When the war finally ended in 1865, the country found itself in a moral depression. The only cure that many could see for the apathy of the country was a return to the camp meeting revivalism of the past. By this time the Methodist church was itself undergoing a period of "progressivism" and change. Ministers in the church were being deeply influenced by evolution. Higher criticism was being introduced into the seminaries. More formal approaches to worship were introduced into churches, including the advent of organs and robed choirs. Fewer Methodist ministers had any interest in camp meeting-style worship, or in preaching the holiness message of the past.

In 1867, more-conservative Methodists and ministers from other Holiness groups began a crusade to save the camp meeting tradition and promote the doctrine of entire sanctification. The group called itself "The National Camp Meeting Association for the Promotion of Christian Holiness." Before the close of the century, dozens of Holiness denominations had been formed from this association, many of which came directly out of the Methodist church. The modern Holiness Movements, in turn, prepared the way for Pentecostalism.

Divine Healing Provided in the Atonement

Blessed be the glorious tidings to a suffering world revealed;

Jesus ever welcomed the sufferers, to His mercy who appealed;

Blessed be the sacred anointing, by the Holy Spirit sealed;

Jesus has atoned for our sickness, and by His stripes we are healed.

Still He bids us bring Him our sickness, for by His stripes we are healed.

Jesus, lay Thine own hand upon us, for by Thy stripes we are healed.

Chorus:

Blessed be the great atonement, to a suff'ring world revealed;

Blessed be the great Physician, for by His stripes we are healed.

This hymn by A.B. Simpson, founder of the Christian and Missionary Alliance (1897), aptly conveys the conviction held by the vast majority of Holiness believers by the close of the 19th century. They believed that the full gospel is one that proclaims Christ as Savior, Sanctifier, Healer, and soon-coming King. Holiness advocates were not the first in the Christian tradition to teach divine healing, but they did provide a theological environment in which this doctrine could flourish. Interestingly, views in the movement about the manner in which God heals tended to be linked to specific views about sanctification. Those who stressed that sanctification occurs instantly tended to emphasize divine healing as an instantaneous work. Those who reflected the Keswickian view of sanctification as a gradual work of grace tended to emphasize that although God may immediately confer healing, its actual manifestation is likely to occur gradually.

Virtually all Holiness groups held that divine healing was a provision of the Atonement that needed to be recovered and restored in the modern church. Healing was definitely a vital part of the ministry of Jesus. Matthew wrote, "Jesus went about all Galilee, teaching in their synagogues, preaching the gospel of the kingdom, and healing all kinds of sickness and all kinds of disease among the people" (4:23). Jesus proclaimed the power of the kingdom of God and embodied that power by healing the sick and casting out demons (12:28). Healings were evidences of Jesus' compassion for the people and His desire to free them from the total effects of sin and evil (8:16, 17).

Healing and the Church. If the Book of Acts portrayed the life of the church as God intended it to function through the ages—and Holiness advocates believed it did—then Acts presented a convincing case for the healing ministry of the church. This book is the story of the continuation of the ministry of Jesus through His apostles and disciples. He had called and given them authority "over unclean spirits, to cast them out, and to heal all kinds of sickness and all kinds of disease" (Matthew 10:1). Healings recorded in the Book of Acts confirmed the preaching of the Word and gave witness to the power of the resurrected Christ.

The Book of James indicates that praying for the sick became an established function of the early church. The sick called for the elders of the church, who anointed them with oil in the name of the Lord. The prayer of faith would heal/save the sick, and the Lord would raise up the sick person. If he or she had committed sins, they were forgiven (5:13-16). One did not have to be an apostle to pray for the sick, for "the effective, fervent prayer of a righteous man avails much" (v. 16).

In time, the sacrament of extreme unction replaced the practice of praying for the sick in the Roman Church. Belief in a generally unalterable order of natural events eventually took precedence over belief in divine intervention and miracles of healing. In the Reformed tradition, divine healing was relegated to the apostolic era and regarded as a temporary gift no longer intended for the church.

In German Pietism, belief in divine healing was resurrected through men like John Albert Bengel and

Johann Christoph Blumhardt. John Wesley's model of grace and salvation emphasizing God's intention to restore all that was lost through the power of sin naturally lent itself to belief in healing and the restoration of health. But it remained for Holiness advocates like Charles Finney, Charles Cullis, W.E. Boardman, Phoebe Palmer, A.B. Simpson, and A.J. Gordon to call attention to the fact that all Christians could claim the promise of divine healing because it is provided through Christ's atonement. As Simpson noted:

> Redemption finds its center in the Cross of our Lord Jesus Christ and there we must look for the fundamental principle of Divine Healing, which rests on the atoning sacrifice. This necessarily follows from the first principle we have stated. If sickness be the result of the Fall, it must be included in the atonement of Christ, which reaches as "far as the curse is found."[16]

Healing and Forgiveness. Simpson's view was consistent with Boardman's, who understood that the restorationist themes of "forgiveness" and "healing" belong together. One of Boardman's favorite scriptures was Psalm 103:2, 3, where the twin motifs are beautifully brought together: "Bless the Lord, O my soul, and forget not all His benefits: who forgives all your iniquities, who heals all your diseases." Belief in healing through the Atonement was also consistent with the James passage: it clearly sets the same basis for the healing of the body as for the forgiveness of sins. Many drew the same connection from the apostle Peter, who wrote, "Who Himself bore our sins in His own body on the tree, that we, having died to sins, might live for righteousness—by whose stripes you were healed" (1 Peter 2:24).[17]

It is not surprising, however, that a vulnerable doctrine such as divine healing would be misunderstood. Some erroneously reasoned that if sickness was part of the curse of sin, then all who were sick and afflicted must be living in sin. Others reasoned that since healing had been provided through the Atonement, any sign of sickness and disease must be due to a lack of faith on the part of the infirm. Any dependence on doctors and medicine was accordingly viewed as a sign of a lack of faith in God's divine provision. In time, such errors would be rectified by a better understanding of biblical teaching. Sickness and suffering would not be assigned to sins committed by the sufferer but to the power of sin introduced into the world through the sin of Adam. It ceased to be a spiritual stigma to go to the doctor and take medicine, as healing advocates realized that God often wills to heal through natural as well as supernatural means. Similarly, those who were not immediately healed did not have to regard it as spiritual failure or lack of faith. They came to realize that the basis of healing is not simply a matter of faith but the sovereign will of God. It was not faith healing but divine healing that Christ provided through the Atonement.

Almost all Pentecostal groups believed in and practiced divine healing as taught in the Holiness Movement. Pentecostals believed, as had their Holiness brethren, that divine healing was a special provision of the Atonement. But they also regarded healing as a manifestation of Pentecostal power. It was one of the "signs and wonders" one could expect to be manifested in the latter-day outpouring of the Holy Spirit.

Pentecostal Eschatology

Pentecostals have always had a special interest in eschatology, the doctrine of last things. They believe that the outpouring of the Holy Spirit is itself a fulfillment of end-time prophecy. For Pentecostals, however, eschatology is more than a series of apocalyptic events. It is an aspect of Pentecostal experience. Eschatology, as Pentecostals know and experience it, tells them who they are as the eschatological people of God living under the new order of the latter rain. It defines their purpose as they seek to fulfill the eschatological mission of preparing the church and the harvest for the second coming of Christ. The mission is accomplished in the power of the Spirit and the restored spiritual gifts.

Christian hope is more than a set of expectations regarding future events. It draws the spiritual power of the future into the present. The fourth Gospel shows us this truth in a beautiful way when John substituted the motif of eternal life for the much-emphasized kingdom-of-God message of the Synoptics. Eternal life, according to John, does not mean simply the extension of life after death. It means a different quality of life has already been introduced by Christ and made available through the Holy Spirit. More than a future event, eternal life is a present spiritual reality. Through the Holy Spirit the Christian already experiences the life and power of the Kingdom. Those in whom the Spirit

dwells already have a taste of the life of the
come. Christians are not merely enduring v
they await a transhistorical salvation. Through
power and presence of the Holy Spirit, they now
have a foretaste of the quality of life they will one
day know in its fullness.

Paul made a similar emphasis in his writings. Joy
and peace in Christ are an eschatological reality that
transcends earthly pleasure and graces the inner life
of the believer (Romans 2:10; 8:6; 14:17; 15:13). These
virtues result from the Christian's relatedness to the
future, not from anything within the present world.
The fruit of the Spirit (love, joy, peace, long-suffering,
kindness, goodness, faithfulness, gentleness, self-con-
trol) identifies the new existence of the believer who is
living in the Spirit (Galatians 5:22, 23).

Life in the Spirit is lived in accordance with the
power and norm of the future. As long as we are in
this world, we will live in the presence of sin, but the
Holy Spirit wills to deliver us from the power of sin
and death. Sin, suffering, and death will be finally
abolished after Christ comes again to complete the
work of redemption (1 Corinthians 15:26, 54-56;
Revelation 21:4). Even now the first installment of
the new life through the Spirit has begun to shape
our attitudes and behavior. Those who live according to the Spirit are no longer dominated by "the law
of sin and death," or the old Adam. The Spirit of life
in Jesus Christ has set us free from the law of sin and
death (Romans 8:2). The Holy Spirit who lives within us opposes sin and carnality. God calls us to holiness and righteousness (1 Corinthians 1:30;
1 Thessalonians 4:7). He calls us to "purify our-

selves from everything that contaminates body and spirit, perfecting holiness out of reverence for God" (2 Corinthians 7:1, *NIV*). Those filled with the Spirit take the same posture toward the world that the Spirit takes because of His holy nature and witness.

Believers have not yet experienced all they will experience in terms of re-creation. That must await the return of Christ and the glorification of the believer. But the indwelling Spirit foreshadows all that is yet to come (Romans 8:23). He is the guarantee (*arrabon*) of our future inheritance and is at the same time an advance installment of it (2 Corinthians 5:5; Ephesians 1:13, 14). The promise of the Spirit is clear. What God has begun in the power of the Spirit, He will complete.

Premillennial Second Coming of Christ

The full-gospel heritage Pentecostals inherited from the Wesleyan-Holiness Movement emphasized the total benefits of the Atonement. The provision included salvation (justification and the new birth), sanctification, and divine healing. Another aspect of that doctrinal tradition centered in a different understanding of end-time events. An important part of the synthesis of the holiness doctrine that Pentecostals would claim for themselves was a premillennial eschatology that maintained the second coming of Christ would precede and prepare the way for the thousand-year reign of Christ on the earth. This represented the changing vision of end-time events in the late 19th century.

The order of future events is outlined in the Bible, but it has been understood in different ways during various periods of church history. In the Old Testament, eschatology was closely bound up with messianic hope. In the New Testament the subject of the endtimes resurfaced and became a dominant theme in the teaching of Jesus and Paul. Jesus addressed the subject in many of His parables. Whole chapters are given over to the theme of endtime events in the Gospels (e.g., Matthew 24; Mark 13; Luke 21). The subject of the end is at the heart of many New Testament books (e.g., 1 and 2 Thessalonians; Revelation).

Historical Influences. After many of the events predicted in the New Testament failed to materialize as early Christians expected, it became common to interpret eschatological events along allegorical lines. Throughout the Middle Ages, there was a tendency to view the Millennium merely as a symbol of the church age—a view known as amillennialism. After the Protestant Reformation in the 16th century, however, emphasis shifted to what is known as a postmillennial view. That is to say, many believed that the Millennium would precede the return of Christ, thus making the expectation of Christ's return less imminent. Those holding this view expected society to be gradually transformed by the power of the gospel so that righteousness would be spread over the earth, preparing the way for the return of Christ and the setting up of His kingdom.

Many Puritans and Pietists expected the fall of Rome and the pope, the conversion of the Jews, and the general betterment of society to result in the latter-day glory of the church. The millennial expectations of holiness advocates generally followed their conviction that Christian perfection could be applied on a social level to the betterment of the world and to the entire sanctification of the church. It was not until after the Civil War that the postmillennial vision of revivalist preachers in America, like Jonathan Edwards and Charles Finney, began to be challenged by a radical turn of historical events and a new understanding of biblical eschatology.[18]

Cultural Influences. The cultural crisis that precipitated the rise of a premillennial view of eschatology was spawned by a number of developments that occurred during the latter half of the 19th century. Darwinism, the rise of biblical criticism, an increase in the number of Catholic and Jewish immigrants to this country, and an increased pessimism about the possibilities of reaching the world with the gospel caused many to reevaluate their view that the world was somehow being prepared for a glorious millennial reign. The direction of the culture seemed to be one of decline, not progress. It was clear to premillennialists that the purpose of the church was not to transform the world but to prepare a "select few" for the return of the Lord.

Meanwhile, the premillennial view was gaining widespread doctrinal acceptance as a result of prophecy conferences taking place throughout the country. D.L. Moody, A.B. Simpson, and A.J. Gordon were all believers in the premillennial second coming of Christ. By the turn of the century virtually all of the great Holiness leaders who exerted a strong influence on Pentecostal doctrine were advocates of premillennial eschatology.

The premillennial perspective, however, tended to

ride the tide of dispensationalism, which was gaining wide acceptance among fundamentalist Christians at about that same time. Dispensationalists held that God deals with the human race in different ways during different periods of time. Some identified as many as seven dispensations when human faith had been tested in light of some specific revelation of God's will. Dispensationalists also had a strong emphasis upon a certain order of future events that were, for the most part, compatible with the way Pentecostals read the Scriptures.

Both believed in the premillennial second coming of Christ, the pretribulation rapture of the church, seven years of Tribulation, the Millennium, the final judgment of the present order, and eternal life for the righteous and eternal punishment for the wicked. Concerning future events, Pentecostals and dispensationalists were fairly comfortable with each other.

The dispensationalists' posture on the gifts of the Spirit and the nature of the church was not compatible with the Pentecostal perspective, however. Dispensationalists taught that there was no real continuity between the people of God in the Old Testament and the church in the New Testament. God's dealings with Israel, they believed, were different from His dealings with the New Testament church that began at Pentecost. More serious, from the Pentecostal point of view, was the Dispensationalists' rejection of miracles and spiritual gifts in the church today. These gifts, they believed, were temporarily granted to the apostolic church but ceased when that age ended.

In the end, fundamentalist dispensationalists who

believed that divine healing, speaking in tongues, and spiritual gifts ceased with the apostles of the New Testament denounced the Pentecostal Movement and the miraculous gifts commonly associated with it.[19] It was an unfortunate break in light of the fact that Pentecostals and fundamentalists share so many of the great evangelical truths of the Bible in common.

The heritage of Pentecostals, then, comes from Scripture and the early church, but it also has deep roots in historical Christianity. Pentecostal Christians rest their faith firmly on the grand truths of the Reformation and in the revival and Holiness movements of the last century. Pentecostals pay homage to a glorious heritage in order to surge forward into a more glorious future in the power of the Spirit.

Questions for Reflection

1. Explain what is meant when we say the Pentecostal Movement, like all true spiritual movements in history, was both a *kairos* and a *chronos* event. Do you agree with this interpretation of the movement? Why, or why not?

2. What did the Protestant reformers recover that is essential to a scriptural understanding of the doctrine of salvation? Why are total depravity and justification through faith alone such vital Christian doctrines?

3. Was John Wesley in essential agreement with Luther and Calvin on the doctrine of salvation? Can you identify significant differences?

4. What does an Arminian believe? How do Arminians differ from Calvinists in their understanding of salvation?

5. How did Wesley distinguish between justification, regeneration, and entire sanctification (or Christian perfection)? What does each represent in the order of salvation? What does each contribute to the restoration of God's image in the lives of Christian believers?

6. Could you explain to another person what Wesley meant by "Christian perfection"? When does one receive it? How does one know he/she has received the experience? What are some common

misconceptions about Wesley's doctrine of Christian perfection?

7. In what way(s) was the Holiness Movement influenced by Wesleyanism? Describe some of the characteristics of the movement.

8. How did divine healing become such an integral part of the full-gospel heritage that Pentecostals inherited from their Holiness forebears? Explain what Pentecostals mean when they say that divine healing is provided for in the Atonement.

9. In what sense is Pentecostal eschatology more than a set of expectations regarding future events? Explain the difference in the premillennial and post-millennial expectations of the second coming of Christ. What factors contributed to the rise of pre-millennialism in the late 19th century? Can you identify the order of future events as most Pentecostals believe they will occur?

Notes

[1]David C. Steinmetz, "The Necessity of the Past," *Theology Today*, vol. 33, no. 2, July 1976, p. 176.

[2]For a fuller treatment of this thesis, see Donald Dayton, *Theological Roots of Pentecostalism* (Grand Rapids: Zondervan Publishing Co., 1987).

[3]John Calvin, *Institutes of the Christian Religion*, I. i. 1.

[4]Roland H. Bainton, *Here I Stand* (Nashville, Tenn.: Abingdon-Cokesbury Press, 1950), p. 65.

[5]Martin Luther, "A Treatise on Christian Liberty," *Works of Martin Luther With Introduction and Notes*, The Philadelphia Edition, vol. 2, (Grand Rapids, Mich.: Baker Book House, 1982), p. 338.

[6]Luther's *The Bondage of the Will* is a profound treatment of this matter.

[7]Wesley taught that prevenient grace creates in us the power to accept or refuse God's offer of salvation. God is at work in all through conscience, which Wesley believed to be a form of prevenient grace. A positive response of the natural person to this grace is not sufficient to bring one to salvation, but it will most likely bring a further gift of grace through the offer of the gospel. Only the grace that comes through the gospel leads to justification. The only way to be justified is by Christ alone. Those unable to hear the gospel in this lifetime, Wesley believed, will be judged by the response they make to the grace they have already received. "No man sins because he has not grace," Wesley said, "but because he does not use the grace which he hath" (*Works*, vol. 6, p. 512). Those who have not heard the Gospel, but who have responded positively to the prevenient grace of Christ through conscience, are like the patriarchs who were justified by their faith in anticipation of Christ. In that intermediate state

of paradise between death and resurrection, Wesley taught, the souls of just men will be made perfect (*Works*, vol. 6, p. 206).

For those interested in the Arminian-Calvinist debate and would like a strong exposition and defense of the Arminian point of view, I recommend Mildred Bangs Wynkoop's *Foundations of Wesleyan-Arminian Theology* (Kansas City, Mo.: Beacon Hill Press, 1967).

[8]*The Standard Sermons of John Wesley*, annotated by E.H. Sugden (London: Epworth Press, 1956), vol. 1, pp. 299-300; cited in Colin William's *John Wesley's Theology Today* (Nashville, Tenn.: Abingdon Press, 1979), p. 99.

[9]Nehemiah Curnock, ed., *The Journal of John Wesley* (London: Epworth Press, 1938), vol. 1, pp. 475-76; cited in Williams, p. 105.

[10]Sermon 85, "On Working Out Our Own Salvation," part 2, section 1, in the Jackson edition of Wesley's *Works*, vol. 6, p. 509; cited in Dayton, p. 46.

[11]See Gordon Rupp, *Principalities and Powers* (London: Epworth Press, 1952), pp. 77ff.

[12]Thomas Jackson, ed., *The Works of John Wesley*, 3rd ed. (London: John Mason, 1829), vol. 11, p. 384; cited in Williams, p. 182.

[13] It is important to note, as Colin Williams points out, that the Christian always falls short of the perfect law of God. Christian perfection, for Wesley, did not mean that one can be perfect with regard to the moral law. It means rather that one is to live in an unbroken relationship to Christ with a constant desire to do His will. See Williams, pp. 182ff.

[14]*Works*, vol. 11, p. 442; cited in Williams, p. 185. Keep in mind that Wesley stressed both the instantaneous gift of perfection, or sanctification, and the gradual nature of

this work of grace. This is not a self-contradictory position but a coherent one that needs to be maintained.

[15]*Works*, vol. 11, pp. 402-403; cited in Williams, p. 188.

[16]A.B. Simpson, *The Gospel of Healing*, rev. ed. (New York: Christian Alliance Publishing, 1915), p. 34; cited in Dayton, p. 128.

[17]See Dayton, p. 125.

[18]*Ibid.*, pp. 160-167.

[19]In 1928, fundamentalists formally renounced Pentecostal doctrines and practices, particularly spiritual gifts and miracles. The resolution by which they disassociated themselves from the entire movement read:

> Whereas, the present wave of modern Pentecostalism, often referred to as the "tongues movement," and the present wave of fanatical and unscriptural healing which is sweeping over the country today, has become a menace in many churches and a real injury to sane testimony of Fundamental Christians,

> Be it resolved that this convention go on record as unreservedly opposed to modern Pentecostalism, including the speaking in unknown tongues, and the fanatical healing known as general healing in the atonement, and the perpetuation of the miraculous sign-healing of Jesus and His apostles, wherein they claim the only reason the church cannot perform these miracles is because of unbelief.

See Vinson Synan, *The Holiness-Pentecostal Movement in the United States* (Grand Rapids: Eerdman's Publishing Co., 1971), pp. 204-206.

BAPTISM
IN THE
HOLY SPIRIT

When the outpouring of the Holy Spirit occurred at the turn of the 20th century, forces were already in motion which would give rise to the Pentecostal Movement. Holiness leaders everywhere were proclaiming a full-gospel message that included salvation, sanctification, healing for the body, and the premillennial second coming of Christ. Some were even using the phrase "baptism in the Holy Spirit" in connection with sanctification and Christian perfection. But there was, as yet, no distinctive doctrine of a "third blessing" experience known as "baptism in the Holy Spirit" with the initial evidence of speaking in other tongues. This doctrine Pentecostals were destined to bequeath to the 20th century and would, more than any other belief, distinguish Pentecostals from their Holiness counterparts.

Luther had recovered in the 16th century the biblical doctrine of salvation by grace alone. In the 18th century Wesley recovered the message of sanctification and passed it on through the influence of the Holiness Movement. But it remained for Pentecostals to recover the importance of Spirit baptism and the power of Pentecost.

Power is virtually synonymous with the Holy Spirit. Jesus told His disciples that they would "receive power" (literally, *dunamis*, from which we get the English word *dynamo*) when the Holy Spirit came on them. This endowment of spiritual power would represent something different from the work of the Spirit by which one is "born of the Spirit" and the Christian life is initiated. It would also be different from the sanctifying grace that the Holy Spirit effects in the lives of Christian believers. Being "filled" or "baptized" in the Holy Spirit would empower believers for Christian witness and service.

The Scriptures teach clearly that God wills to empower all whom He calls and commissions into His service. God never calls to Christian service without the benefit of spiritual power. When Christ sent His disciples forth, He gave them authority over all that they would encounter. Luke says, "He called His twelve disciples together and gave them power and authority over all demons, and to cure diseases. He sent them to preach the kingdom of God and to heal the sick" (Luke 9:1, 2). The power with which Jesus initiated the Kingdom was given to the Twelve and later promised to all who would continue Jesus' ministry in the world:

You are witnesses of these things. Behold, I send the Promise of My Father upon you; but tarry in the city of Jerusalem until you are endued with power from on high (Luke 24:48, 49).

You shall receive power when the Holy Spirit has come upon you; and you shall be witnesses to Me in Jerusalem, and in all Judea and Samaria, and to the end of the earth (Acts 1:8).

Being endued, or clothed, with power for witness and service is never presented as an optional experience for Christian believers in the New Testament. All believers comprise an extension of His body in the world through the power of the Holy Spirit. The church before Pentecost lacked motivation and power. Essentially, it was an inactive church because it was not yet fully equipped for its mission. The church needed the power of the Holy Spirit to fulfill the Great Commission. When the New Testament church received the initial enduement of power at Pentecost, it was transformed immediately into a witnessing and serving church. The power of the Holy Spirit was, and continues to be, necessary for the fulfillment of the church's mission in the world.

Spirit Baptism in Church Tradition

An examination of the past has importance for Pentecostals because the doctrine they are most often associated with, the baptism in the Holy Spirit, has often been dismissed as some kind of unfounded or fringe belief. There is, however, a continuity of belief running throughout the Christian tradition that holds to a distinctive operation or gift of the Holy

Spirit, subsequent to (following or coming after) conversion and referred to as the baptism in the Holy Spirit. The supreme authority for doctrine, of course, is Scripture and not tradition. But one is reminded of John Wesley's observation that something must be wrong with our exegesis of Scripture if both experience and tradition contradict it. One cannot simply ignore 2,000 years of church tradition in interpreting the Scriptures. An examination of the past is as essential to responsible theological work for Pentecostals as it is for those in other theological traditions.

Roman Catholic Perspective and Subsequence

Pentecostals and Roman Catholics have significant disagreements on many theological matters. They disagree, for example, about the nature of the church, the meaning of the sacraments, the papacy, Mariology, purgatory, and a number of other dogmas that have historically separated Roman Catholics and Protestants. But there is one important area pertaining to the doctrine of subsequence that should not be minimized or overlooked. Both Pentecostals and Roman Catholics hold the view that there is a special work of the Holy Spirit in the life of the Christian that is subsequent to the new birth.

Early in Roman Catholic tradition a distinction was drawn between the work of the Spirit whereby one is converted and becomes a Christian and a subsequent work of the Holy Spirit whereby one receives the fullness of the Spirit in accordance with the Acts 2:4 pattern. This distinction was made in the Catholic understanding of the sacraments of baptism and confirmation. In Catholic understanding of these two sacraments, salvation was presented in two stages. To be sure, the Catholic understanding of baptismal grace was far removed from an Evangelical understanding of conversion. Further, Catholic understanding of confirmation would hardly qualify as an acceptable substitute for the Pentecostal understanding of baptism in the Holy Spirit. But these obvious differences should not obscure the fact that early church tradition recognized and allowed for two definitive works of grace wrought by the Holy Spirit in the life of the Christian believer.

William J. O'Shea of the Catholic University of America explains the Catholic understanding of these two separate, yet related, works of the Spirit:

> In the life of Christ there were two anointings by the Spirit. The first was at the moment of the Incarnation; that one established Him as the Son of God. . . . By this anointing which is the hypostatic union, Jesus was constituted king and priest at the same time. It was His royal and priestly consecration.
>
> The other anointing took place when He was baptized in the Jordan. At that moment He accepted his mission as "suffering servant" and Messiah-Redeemer. He was anointed then as the great Agent of the divine plan of salvation. This was His prophetical anointing.
>
> These two separate, yet related, anointings must be reproduced in the life of the Christian. The first anointing of the Spirit takes place at baptism, making him the adopted son of God. The second takes

place at confirmation, when the Spirit descends upon him again to make him a prophet, to equip him with the gifts he needs to enable him to live fully the life of an adopted son, and to fulfill his mission in the Church.

Jesus was anointed with the Spirit at the time of His baptism, but it was at Pentecost that the apostles were anointed by the Spirit. The Spirit we receive in confirmation is the Spirit of Pentecost.[1]

From the Pentecostal's point of view, what is significant in the Catholic understanding of this two-stage operation of the Spirit is its admission that there is biblical precedence for a special work of the Holy Spirit that completes and perfects the Spirit's work in regeneration and that this work can be exegetically traced to Pentecost. The aim of this second work of the Spirit, Catholics believe, is to conform the believer to Christ; but they also see it as a special anointing for Christian witness and service. Like the Wesleyan doctrine of sanctification, the Catholic doctrine of confirmation prescribes an experience of the Spirit subsequent to regeneration and represents a moral completion of character.

Protestant Development and Tradition

The 16th-century Protestant Reformers rejected the Catholic sacrament of confirmation, so all emphasis on a definitive work of the Holy Spirit subsequent to the Spirit's work in regeneration disappeared for a while. John Calvin labeled the Catholic teaching of confirmation "horrible blasphemies" and rejected the Catholic exegesis of scriptures supporting a work of grace subsequent to the new birth (e.g., Acts 8:14-17; 19:1, 2).[2] In the 17th century a renewed emphasis on a second and subsequent work of the Spirit emerged again in the form of the Puritan experience of assurance, but it was not until the 18th century that the two-stage perspective was again raised to doctrinal status—this time by John Wesley.[3]

Wesley's emphasis on entire sanctification is well known. The experience of holiness, or perfection in love, was, in his thinking, a divine gift subsequent to justification. This second work of grace was believed to be related to the Spirit's work in justification and regeneration and was understood to be the completion of what they anticipated—a holy life. Unlike the Reformers, Catholics and Wesleyans alike acknowledged a definitive work of the Holy Spirit subsequent to conversion. Scholars in both traditions cited the same passages in the Book of Acts to distinguish the fullness of the Spirit from the "new birth" in the Spirit. Both associated the fullness of the Spirit with the completion or perfection of character begun in regeneration.[4]

Neither tradition, however, associated this second work of the Spirit with Spirit baptism, or with what some in the Holiness Movement called "baptism in the Holy Spirit." The Holiness Movement in the 19th century brought Spirit baptism terminology into prominence. The "Higher Life" teaching in British holiness circles emphasized a distinction between justification by faith, through which one is delivered from the *penalty* of sin, and a second work of sanctification, through which one is delivered from the *power* of sin. This second work of the Spirit was sometimes called "the baptism of the Holy Ghost," but there was never any mention of speaking in tongues as the initial evidence of the experience. In the Holiness Movement the experience of what was called the "baptism in the Holy Spirit" was associated with cleansing and sanctification by some. Holiness advocates coming from a more reformed perspective eventually saw the purpose of the experience as empowerment for witness and service.[5]

In America the phrase "baptism in the Holy Spirit" was first used at Oberlin College by Asa Mahan and Charles Finney in connection with Oberlin perfectionism. After the Civil War there was a rapid shift from the language of "Christian perfectionism" to "baptism in the Holy Spirit." Everything from camp meetings to choirs were described as "Pentecostal." There were "Pentecostal sermons," "Pentecostal testimonies," and "Pentecostal churches."[6] Prominent Holiness churches carried the name "Pentecostal" as part of their official name. The Church of the Nazarene was originally called the Pentecostal Church of the Nazarene. In Scotland, Nazarene congregations called themselves the Pentecostal Church of Scotland.

It is important to remember that Holiness advocates were using the phrase "baptism in the Holy Spirit" and the term "Pentecostal" in reference to the work of the Holy Spirit in sanctification, and there was no connection between the use of Pentecostal terminology and speaking in tongues. But forces giving rise to the Pentecostal Movement were definitely in motion. Holiness leaders had already aroused new interest in spiritual gifts by teaching that they should still operate in the church. Interest in divine healing was particularly strong. Toward the close of the 19th century, R.A. Torrey was helping shift emphasis away from the Holiness teaching that the baptism in the Holy Spirit is to cleanse from sin to an emphasis on power for witness and service. His belief was based principally on Luke 24:49 and Acts 1:5, 8.[7] The only thing that seemed to be missing was the actual outpouring of the Spirit itself and the initial physical evidence of speaking in other tongues as the Spirit gives utterance.

The Pentecostal Distinctive

While teachings on holiness and sanctification as a work of grace separate from conversion preceded the Pentecostal Movement, other teachings were distinctively Pentecostal. One was the doctrine that tongues is the initial evidence of a distinct experience that Scripture calls the "baptism in the Holy Spirit." The Pentecostal outpourings at Camp Creek, Topeka, and Azusa Street were accompanied by what seemed to the participants a strange phenomenon of speaking in tongues. When those who received the experience turned to the Scriptures for an explanation, they discovered that the same phenomenon had accompanied Spirit baptism in Acts. Based on what they discovered from the pattern in Acts (chapters 2, 8, 10, 19), Pentecostals concluded that speaking in tongues must be the initial physical evidence of a person's receiving this distinct spiritual experience. The decision to elevate this belief to doctrinal status was what gave theological distinctiveness to the Pentecostal Movement of the 20th century.

Most early Pentecostals came out of, or were deeply influenced by, the Holiness tradition which already stressed two crisis experiences: conversion and sanctification. Pentecostals from that tradition were convinced that Spirit baptism was really a third work of divine grace. Virtually all of the early Pentecostal bodies emphasized three crisis experiences: salvation, sanctification, and baptism in the Holy Spirit. The exceptions were those Pentecostals who were more deeply influenced by Reformed theology that allowed for only two crisis experiences—conversion and baptism in the Holy Spirit, combined with a gradual form of sanctification.[8]

To those remaining within the Holiness tradition, the new Pentecostalism with its "tongues-speaking" experience could only appear to be some kind of "holiness heresy." Holiness advocates were, in many cases, the archcritics of the Pentecostal experience. This new adversarial attitude was exemplified by the Nazarenes, who promptly dropped the word *Pentecostal* from their official church name lest they be identified with the emerging Pentecostal Movement and their doctrine of tongues.[9] Those in mainline Protestant churches viewed Pentecostals with even more suspicion, for there was no place in their theology for a definitive work of the Holy Spirit subsequent to regeneration.

The Pentecostal Doctrine

Many traditions are represented in the Pentecostal Movement. As one would expect in a situation so rich and diverse, not all Pentecostals believe and teach exactly the same thing about the baptism in the Holy Spirit. Yet, there is a common body of belief about the experience which virtually all classical Pentecostals share.[10] It is to this body of common belief that we want to focus attention. If the Pentecostal heritage is to be assessed and appreciated, it ought to be on the basis of what Pentecostals believe and publicly state about their experience. With this in mind, we turn to the first tenet to which all Pentecostals subscribe.

Spirit Baptism Is a Biblically Based Experience

• The prophecy of John the Baptist that appears in all four of the Gospels was that Jesus would baptize believers in the Holy Spirit. "I indeed baptize you with water unto repentance," John said, "but He [Jesus] . . . will baptize you with the Holy Spirit and fire" (Matthew 3:11).

• The expectation that Jesus would baptize in the Holy Spirit was obviously well known, for it is mentioned no less than six times in the New Testament (Matthew 3:11; Mark 1:8; Luke 3:16; John 1:33: Acts 1:5; 11:16).

• Some three years after the announcement by John, Jesus personally promised to baptize His disciples with the Holy Spirit: "He commanded them not to depart from Jerusalem, but to wait for the Promise of the Father, 'which,' He said, 'you have heard from Me; for John truly baptized with water, but you shall be baptized with the Holy Spirit not many days from now'" (Acts 1:4, 5).

• Shortly after this the promise was fulfilled when the 120 disciples of Jesus were filled with the Holy

Spirit in the Upper Room in Jerusalem. All of them, the Scripture says, were "filled with the Holy Spirit and began to speak with other tongues, as the Spirit gave them utterance" (Acts 2:4).

• Peter recognized that the Holy Spirit poured out on Cornelius and his household was the same baptism John had prophesied about, Jesus had promised, and the 120 disciples had received at Pentecost (Acts 11:15-17). "Then I remembered the word of the Lord, how He said, 'John indeed baptized with water, but you shall be baptized with the Holy Spirit' " (v. 16).

This is the same experience contemporary Pentecostals claim when they speak of being "baptized in the Holy Spirit." Pentecostals speak about Spirit baptism with conviction because they know about this biblical truth through experience.

To the Pentecostal the truth of the Spirit baptism is more than a simple statement of fact. It is more than orthodox teaching, a tradition, or a ritual act such as water baptism or confirmation administered by an ecclesiastical institution. Spirit baptism is an "experience," a direct contact with the presence and power of God. Pentecostals have refocused attention on Spirit baptism in terms of experience, not for the purpose of exalting experience but in the interest of faithfully communicating the essence of this biblically based reality.

New Testament scholars who do not claim the experience for themselves recognize that Spirit baptism in the New Testament was an experienced reality. Eduard Schweizer notes that "long before the Spirit was an article of doctrine, it was a fact of experience in the primitive church."[11] Lesslie Newbigin, another prominent theologian, comments that "most Christians today would not likely be asked the same question that the apostle asked the converts of Apollos in Acts 19:2: 'Did you receive the Holy Spirit when you believed?' Modern successors would be more likely to ask, 'Did you believe what we teach?' Or, 'Were the hands that were laid on you our hands?' " The reason for such questions, Newbigin suggests, is that since the first century Spirit baptism has been identified in many traditions with the sacraments of baptism and confirmation.[12] Pentecostals, however, boldly witness to an experience with God that has anointed them for witness and service because they have personally experienced the presence and life of the Spirit.

Spirit Baptism Is a Promised Gift

• At the Feast of Tabernacles, Jesus promised the Spirit would be given to those who believed on Him and thirsted for (desired) the water He would give. "'If anyone thirsts, let him come to Me and drink. He who believes in Me, as the Scripture has said, out of his heart will flow rivers of living water.' But this He spoke concerning the Spirit, whom those believing in Him would receive; for the Holy Spirit was not yet given, because Jesus was not yet glorified" (John 7:37-39).

• Later, Jesus commissioned His disciples and commanded them to stay in Jerusalem until they received the power of the Holy Spirit. He reminded them again that the Holy Spirit was a promised gift: "Behold, I send the Promise of My Father upon you;

but tarry in the city of Jerusalem until you are endued with power from on high" (Luke 24:49).

• In his sermon at Pentecost, Peter stressed to his hearers that what they had received was the promised gift from the Father (Acts 2:33). He reminded them that this promised gift was available to their children and to all who are afar off in time (v. 39).

• Paul's references to the Holy Spirit also emphasized the element of promise, connecting the promise of the Spirit with the promise of faith through Abraham. The Holy Spirit, Paul said, has sealed what was promised and is a guarantee of what God still has in store for Christians (2 Corinthians 1:22; 5:5; Ephesians 1:13, 14; see also Romans 8:16, 17, 23).

In the Old Testament the Holy Spirit was the promised sign of the age to come. In the New Testament the Spirit was the recognized sign that the promised age had indeed broken through in the power of the Holy Spirit.

The Holy Spirit was poured out at Pentecost, then, because the Spirit had been promised. The church did not receive the Spirit because it had somehow merited the Spirit's favor but because it was open and receptive to the promised gift. Simon the sorcerer tried to buy the gift of the Spirit with money but was rebuked by Peter who, on another occasion, was astonished that God had poured out the Spirit as freely on Gentiles as He had on the Jews (cf. Acts 8:20; 11:15-18). The fact that the Holy Spirit is a promised gift does not mean, however, that there are no conditions to one's receiving the gift. None of us fully understand the intricate relation between the working of God's free grace and the necessary movement of man's free will, but the comments of J. Rodman Williams on the subject seem particularly relevant:

> There exists a beautiful harmony between God's free action in the Spirit and our openness to it. The Spirit is a gift and therefore cannot be bought; consequently, there is no earning of the Spirit by any amount of prayers, vigils, and the like. The Spirit moves freely and cannot be compelled or coerced by any human contrivance—no matter how astutely performed. But for the very reason that the Spirit acts graciously in freedom, He will not grant a gift where it is not wanted or asked for, nor will He break through barriers that resist His coming. Thus only the open and expectant, the eager and hungry, the askers and seekers (not because of what they do but because of their readiness) receive God's blessing.[13]

It was clearly God's will for the Holy Spirit to be poured out upon the church. Still, the church had to be receptive to the promised gift. Evil spirits seek to impose themselves on the unwary, but not the Spirit of God. He never dwells in a temple where He is not welcome. Promise does not imply human passivity nor divine determination to impose what is not desired and yielded to.

Self-surrender and obedience, as expressions of faith, are still the requisite conditions for the reception of the Spirit. The Spirit can and will move freely and graciously where He finds no resistance. Pride, in all of its subtle forms, is still the chief obstacle in our quest for the Spirit-filled life. The Pentecostal jargon of "giving up" and "letting go" is still important in what it signifies: the necessity of human readiness and cooperation with the Holy Spirit. As Karl Barth put it, "Only where the Spirit is sighed, cried, and prayed for does he become present and newly active."[14]

Spirit Baptism Is Not Regeneration

It has already been emphasized that the baptism in the Holy Spirit is an experience distinct from and subsequent to the work of the Spirit in regeneration and sanctification. It is certainly true that one could not possibly be saved, or "born again," apart from the work of the Holy Spirit, but the work of the Spirit in Spirit baptism must not be confused with the work of the Spirit in regeneration and/or sanctification. This doctrine of subsequence, Pentecostals believe, is plainly taught in Scripture.

The apostles were obviously regenerate men before they were baptized in the Holy Spirit at Pentecost. The Scriptures indicate in a number of ways that they were already redemptively united with Christ.

• Who could doubt that the disciples were converted before Pentecost when Jesus clearly stated that they had received His word and kept it (John 17:8)? Unconverted men do not receive the Word of God and keep it.

• At the Passover Feast, Jesus announced that all of His disciples were clean except Judas Iscariot (John 13:10).

• The disciples were told that their names were written in heaven and that they ought to rejoice in this knowledge (Luke 10:17-20).

• The fact that our Lord prayed that Peter's faith might not fail him is proof enough that Peter was not an unbeliever (Luke 22:32). The same Peter who confessed his personal belief in Jesus Christ as the Son of the living God at Caesarea (Matthew 16:16) was later filled with the Holy Spirit in the Upper Room in Jerusalem and became the spokesman for the disciples at Pentecost (Acts 2).

Acts 2. To dispel any doubt that there is a special baptism in the Holy Spirit distinct from the work of the Spirit in regeneration, one need only consider the experiences of the early Christians recorded in Acts. Four separate passages in the Book of Acts describe an experience in which Christian believers received the baptism in the Holy Spirit. Acts 2 is the most talked-about and the most well-known.

Acts 8. In chapter 8 we read of believers who had been won to Jesus Christ through the preaching of Philip. They had even been baptized in water. When news reached Jerusalem of these converts, Peter and John went immediately to Samaria and prayed for them to receive the Holy Spirit. Although these Samaritans had been converted and baptized in the name of the Lord Jesus, the Holy Spirit had not yet fallen on any of them. When Peter and John laid their hands on them, they received the Holy Spirit (vv. 15-17). The fact that this baptism in the Spirit was subsequent to their commitment to Jesus Christ is an undeniable truth of Scripture.

Acts 10. In Acts 10 we read of a Gentile man named Cornelius who lived in Caesarea. He feared God, gave liberally to the needy, and prayed; but he was not yet a Christian believer. While Peter preached the Word of God to Cornelius and his household, the Holy Spirit fell on them and they began to speak in tongues. Jewish Christians who had accompanied Peter to Cornelius' house were amazed at what they saw and heard, but they could not doubt the Gentiles' experience with God, because they heard them speaking in tongues and extolling God (vv. 44-48). Unlike the Samaritans, these Caesareans had obviously been simultaneously converted and filled with the Holy Spirit for they were subsequently baptized in water.

Two important truths are revealed through this experience. First, Jewish believers now knew that the gift of the Spirit was for Gentiles as well as for Jews, for they heard them speak in tongues just as they had on the Day of Pentecost. Second, it is also evident that although Spirit baptism is a gift distinct from and subsequent to conversion, this does not mean it has to be a chronologically separate experience. Believers who are open and receptive to the truth of the Word can receive their baptism in the Spirit when they believe.

Acts 19. In Acts 19 we read of some Ephesians who had believed but had not yet received the Holy Spirit. Paul specifically asked these believers if they had received the Holy Spirit when they believed (v. 2). This implies that it is possible to believe in Christ without receiving the fullness of the Spirit. On hearing that they had not, Paul laid hands on them and they received the Holy Spirit. They spoke with tongues and prophesied (v. 6). The question Paul asked of the Ephesians is one that still needs to be asked of Christians today: "Did you receive the Holy Spirit when you believed?"

Spirit Baptism Is Empowerment

Why does one need to be filled with the Holy Spirit? What is the purpose of this experience? These are serious questions that deserve serious answers. Note first that being filled with the Spirit is not an option of the believer. Christ did not suggest that this might be a good thing to do. Rather, He commanded His disciples to wait in Jerusalem until they were endued with power from on high. Spirit baptism is for all who are redemptively united to Christ. Being filled with the Spirit is the believer's spiritual equipment for taking up Christ's vocation in power. It is not an experience that happens to an institution. Institutions will be affected, and their members will be more effective when they are filled with the Spirit, but Spirit baptism is an experience that is profoundly personal. It pleases the Father, Luke tells us, to give the Holy Spirit to those who seek Him (Luke 11:13).

Jesus referred to the Holy Spirit as the "Spirit of truth" (John 16:13), but He did not mean that the Holy Spirit would represent some new truth. The purpose of the Holy Spirit would be to guide the church into the full truth about the historic Jesus. It is in this sense that the Holy Spirit seeks to glorify Him (v. 14). The purpose of the Holy Spirit in the church today is not to give us new truth, but to make the truth we already have through the Word alive and operational. Truths neatly organized and rationalized are not enough. Truth has a way of losing its potency when it is not set aflame by the Holy Spirit. He enables us to see old truths in a new and more powerful way.

We must not think of the Holy Spirit as offering us or giving us "more" than we already have in Christ. The Holy Spirit is the "Spirit of Christ" poured out in a new way. As J. Rodman Williams aptly puts it:

> To be "filled" with the Spirit is not so much to have something "more" as it is to be in the new, wonderful, and at times fearful situation of having the Spirit of God break into the whole round of existence and pervade it all. As a result of this—yes, explosion— what may be violent at the beginning can become the steady and driving power of a mighty dynamo—the Spirit of the living God.[15]

It has already been noted that the purpose of Spirit baptism was not to unite Jesus' disciples to Him in a redemptive way or to make them holier than the cleansing provided through the shed blood of Calvary. The purpose of Pentecost was to empower Jesus' disciples for the task of continuing His work in the world. Jesus had accomplished the will of the Father in the power of the Holy Spirit. Believers would, in turn, become the extension of Christ and bear witness to Him through this same Spirit. What God had begun in the power of the Holy Spirit could not possibly be fulfilled through the arm of the flesh. The church would bear witness to Christ and His ministry through the Spirit just as Christ had borne witness to the Father in the power of the Holy Spirit (Luke 24:47-49; Acts 1:8). The apostolic church remained inactive, even after the resurrection and postresurrection appearances of Christ, until it was empowered by the Holy Spirit for the fulfillment of its mission. When the disciples were filled with the Holy Ghost on the Day of

Pentecost, they were equipped by the Spirit to be Christ's witnesses in word and deed.

Power, *dunamis*, has always been the striking characteristic of the Holy Spirit. In the power of the Holy Spirit, Jesus ministered and performed His mighty works. In this same *dunamis* the Christian community in Acts bore witness to Christ (4:31). They did great wonders and miraculous signs (2:43; 5:12; 6:5, 8; 14:3; 15:12). They healed the sick and cast out evil spirits (8:6, 7). Pentecostals believe in the continuity of this power. It extends to the present age. Unlike those who claim this miraculous power ceased with the apostolic times, Pentecostals believe there is an inseparable, ongoing link between anointed witness and the working of miracles. God has always confirmed His word with signs and wonders. Those born again of the Spirit are commissioned by the Lord to fulfill the ministry of Christ through this same power.

The Spirit's work cannot be humanly prescribed or ordered to fit preexisting conditions. The way in which the Spirit works does not always please our personal tastes or values. He works as He wills to fulfill the purpose of God. Unfortunately, many Christians are not willing to have their ideas exploded or their predictable patterns of worship and lifestyle radically changed. This sometimes occurs when the Holy Spirit is welcomed without reservation into one's life and into the life of the church.

How many in Christendom feel comfortable about communicating with God in the language of the Spirit? How many are willing to allow the Spirit to inspire their faith to the degree that they would lay hands on the incurably ill and declare their healing? How many lives today are marked by the love, joy, and peace that accompanies the Spirit's living presence? The strange world of the Spirit is much too radical for many in Christendom. They speak of their desire for the special presence and power of the Holy Spirit in the church, but what they really want is a domesticated Spirit safely brought under the control of preexisting patterns and expectations. The operation of the Spirit in the church is always a matter of God's free grace.

Those who truly desire the movement of the Holy Spirit in the church today as He moved in the apostolic church must be open and prepared for the free flow of the Spirit. Pentecostal believers have traditionally been characterized by this kind of radical openness to God. It is a crucial part of their spiritual heritage which must never be lost.

One should know, however, that the Holy Spirit does not create confusion and disorder. The power of the Spirit is never manifested to exalt an individual but to glorify Christ and to build up the community of faith. The Spirit who inspires the more obvious signs of His presence in the church also inspires the more simple and humble acts of service that bear witness to Christ and bring glory to God. Gifts of "helps" and "serving" are as important to the operation of the body of Christ as the gift of tongues, healings, or miracles. In Romans 12 and 1 Corinthians 13, Paul emphasized that love must govern the exercise of all spiritual gifts:

Having then gifts differing according to the grace that is given to us, let us use them: if prophecy, let us prophesy in proportion to our faith; or ministry, let us use it in our ministering; he who teaches, in teaching; he who exhorts, in exhortation; he who gives, with liberality; he who leads, with diligence; he who shows mercy, with cheerfulness.

Let love be without hypocrisy. Abhor what is evil. Cling to what is good. Be kindly affectionate to one another with brotherly love, in honor giving preference to one another; not lagging in diligence, fervent in spirit, serving the Lord; rejoicing in hope, patient in tribulation, continuing steadfastly in prayer; distributing to the needs of the saints, given to hospitality (Romans 12:6-13).

Speaking in Tongues

There is, of course, much more to Pentecostalism than speaking in tongues. But since this has always been such a striking feature of Pentecostal doctrine and practice, and a much-misunderstood phenomenon, it is important to state what Pentecostals believe about the subject.

Pentecostals believe that authentic experiences with God result in certainties, not doubts. The apostolic church could speak with boldness about the things they had experienced because they were personally convinced that these things were true. An experience with God that offers assurance and certainty is necessary for all who would give witness to the world with confidence and conviction. God has historically provided outward empirical signs of the inner workings of His grace.

Under the old covenant, circumcision was a constant reminder to the Jewish male that he was a member of the covenant and shared in the promises of God to the covenant community. In the New Testament, water baptism became the outward sign of the new covenant relation. Should it seem strange, then, that God would attach the outward empirical sign of tongues to the gift of Spirit baptism, particularly when the sign so appropriately bespeaks its own significance for the witnessing community?

When the Holy Spirit was poured out at the turn of the 20th century, many Pentecostals were not sure themselves about the meaning of tongues. They had experienced the phenomenon but were not quite sure what to make of it. As they studied Scriptures and committed the matter to prayer, they became convinced that tongues were the initial physical evidence of the baptism in the Holy Spirit. Scriptures such as Acts 2:4; 10:44-46; 19:1-7; and, to their minds, 8:14-24 provided sufficient evidence. After the Azusa Street revival this conviction was raised to doctrinal status by most classical Pentecostals. This doctrinal distinctive, more than any other theological tenet, separated Pentecostals from the main body of the Holiness Movement, which had otherwise provided the infrastructure upon which the gestalt of Pentecostal doctrine had been built.

In the early days of the Movement, many Pentecostals were uncertain as to how to distinguish between speaking in tongues as the initial physical evidence of the baptism in the Holy Spirit and the gift of tongues (*charisma*) mentioned in 1 Corinthians 12. Through a careful study of Scripture, Pentecostals soon concluded that there are two kinds of tongues.

One is a sign to the believer (the initial evidence of the baptism in the Holy Ghost); the other, a gift to be used in public worship for the edification of the church. They are no different in sound, but they are different in function.

The gift of tongues mentioned in 1 Corinthians 12 is given for public worship and requires interpretation so that those who hear may be edified. When interpreted, the gift of tongues may also serve as a sign to unbelievers, just as the strange tongues of foreigners were a sign of God's judgment on the disobedient nation of Israel (1 Corinthians 14:21, 22). The experience of tongues one receives in Spirit baptism, on the other hand, certifies to the believer that the Holy Spirit indwells that person in a special way for the purpose of being Christ's witness in the world. This so-called devotional tongue edifies only the speaker and is intended more for private than for public worship.

Believers, however, should never be encouraged to seek for a "tongues experience" but for the fullness of God's presence and power in their lives. When this happens, the proper certification of the Spirit's presence will occur naturally. Pentecostals do not teach that speaking in tongues is the only evidence of Spirit baptism. In fact, they do not even teach that it is the most important evidence. They simply believe it is the initial (beginning) physical evidence of the baptism in the Holy Spirit, in accordance with the biblical pattern of Acts 2:4; 10:44-46; and 19:1-7. The surest sign that one is living in the power of the Holy Spirit on a daily basis is the lordship of Jesus Christ in his or her life (John 16:13-15;

1 Corinthians 12:1-3). A life lived by the law of love truly glorifies God and is the surest sign of the Spirit's presence (1 Corinthians 13:1-3; 14:1).

Some early Pentecostals were convinced that the purpose for the gift of tongues (1 Corinthians 12) was to enable those who received this gift to supernaturally speak in languages they had not previously learned in order to facilitate the preaching of the gospel in foreign lands. This fascination with xenoglossy (the ability to speak an unlearned foreign language) actually led a number of missionaries to leave for foreign lands not knowing the native language but convinced that the Holy Spirit would enable them to speak it when they arrived. Some disappointing experiences and a more careful study of the Scriptures, however, soon convinced Pentecostals that this was not the purpose of the gift of tongues.[16]

The practice of speaking in tongues in public worship should not be forbidden or despised in the church (1 Corinthians 14:39). One should be aware, however, that this gift, like any other, can be easily abused. It must always be practiced in accordance with the spiritual instructions given by Paul in 1 Corinthians 14:27, 28. In the Corinthian church spiritual gifts were being misused because the Corinthians were given to excess and lacked proper spiritual guidance. In order to correct these abusive and disruptive practices, Paul admonished the church to follow three basic principles:

1. Recognize the diversity of spiritual gifts that God has placed in the church. Speaking in tongues is never more important, and sometimes less important, than other gifts that need to be operated in the

church (1 Corinthians 12).

2. Understand that the law of love is supreme in the church. Without love, the exercising of spiritual gifts profits nothing (1 Corinthians 13).

3. Establish the priority of congregational edification over personal edification, or receiving a "blessing" (1 Corinthian 14). When these spiritual principles are followed, there will always be divine order in the church.

Questions for Reflection

1. For what purpose was the Holy Spirit poured out on the church on the Day of Pentecost? Why do Christian believers today need to be baptized in the Holy Spirit?

2. Explain what is meant by the doctrine of subsequence? How is this doctrine supported by church tradition and by experience?

3. How is the Pentecostal understanding of Spirit baptism different from the way in which the phrase "baptism in the Holy Spirit" was used in the Holiness tradition?

4. How would you explain to a non-Pentecostal the significance of the claim that (a) Spirit baptism is a biblically based experience; (b) Spirit baptism is a promised gift; (c) Spirit baptism is not regeneration; (d) Spirit baptism is empowerment for witness and service?

5. Describe what Pentecostals mean when they say that speaking in other tongues is the initial physical evidence of the baptism in the Holy Spirit. What are some common misconceptions about speaking in tongues?

6. Distinguish between tongues as the initial physical evidence of Spirit baptism and the gift of tongues Paul alluded to in 1 Corinthians 12. How do they differ in function?

Notes

[1]William J. O'Shea, *Sacraments of Initiation* (Englewood Cliffs, N.J.: Prentice-Hall, 1965), p. 63. For similar views on confirmation, see Karl Ranner's *A New Baptism in the Spirit: Confirmation Today* and the chapter "The Universal Call to Holiness in the Church" in *The Sixteen Documents of Vatican II.*

[2]John Calvin, *Commentary on the Book of Acts, vol. 2* (Grand Rapids: Eerdmans, 1949), p. 211. Calvin's views established the pattern for the Reformed tradition.

[3]James D.G. Dunn, "Spirit Baptism and Pentecostalism," *Scottish Journal of Theology,* no. 23 (November 1970), p. 397.

[4]Lawrence W. Wood, "Thoughts Upon the Wesleyan Doctrine of Entire Sanctification With Special Reference to the Roman Catholic Doctrine of Confirmation," *Wesleyan Journal of Theology,* no. 15 (Spring 1980), pp. 91-92.

[5]Dunn, p. 400.

[6]Donald W. Dayton, "From 'Christian Perfection' to the 'Baptism of the Holy Ghost,'" *Aspects of Pentecostal-Charismatic Origins,* Vinson Synan, ed. (Plainfield, N.J.: Logos International, 1975), p. 47.

[7]R.A. Torrey gave the doctrine of Spirit baptism special emphasis in his books *The Baptism With the Holy Spirit* (1897) and *The Person and Work of the Holy Spirit* (1910). But Torrey moved away from the "purity" theme of the Holiness tradition and emphasized that the baptism of the Holy Spirit was for the purpose of empowering for service. Torrey's emphasis was more congenial to the Calvinistic wing of revivalism.

[8]The Church of God, the Pentecostal Holiness Church, and the Church of God in Christ stressed three crisis experiences. Pentecostal groups that were established

later (e.g., the Assemblies of God in 1914 and the International Church of the Foursquare Gospel in 1927) adopted the "finished work" doctrine that assigned sanctification to the act of conversion (i.e., no crisis experience of sanctification), but believed in a gradual growth of sanctifying grace after conversion.

[9]Alma White, W.B. Godbey, G. Campbell Morgan, R.A. Torrey, H.A. Ironside, H.J. Stolee, and Beverly Carradine were outspoken critics of Pentecostalism and "tongues." It should be pointed out, however, that not all traditional Pentecostals insisted on tongues as the evidence of Spirit baptism. T.B. Barrett, the father of European Pentecostalism, maintained that many have had mighty baptisms without the sign of tongues. For a discussion of Barrett and his views, see N. Bloch-Hoell's published dissertation, *The Pentecostal Movement.*

[10]Minor differences among Pentecostals are too numerous to mention. The major deviance occurred in 1914 when a non-Trinitarian element emerged under the name of the "oneness" or "Jesus Only" group. The United Pentecostal Church, with its black affiliate, the Pentecostal Assemblies of the World, is the largest oneness body.

[11]See Schweizer's article on *pneuma* in Kittel's *Theological Wordbook of the New Testament, vol. VI,* p. 394.

[12]Lesslie Newbigin, *The Household of God: Lectures on the Nature of the Church* (New York: Friendship Press, 1954), p. 95.

[13]J. Rodman Williams, *The Era of the Spirit* (Plainfield, N.J.: Logos International, 1971), p. 62.

[14]Karl Barth, *Evangelical Theology,* Glover Foley, trans. (New York: Doubleday and Co., 1964), p. 52.

[15]Williams, p. 55.

[16]The initial fascination with xenoglossy among Pentecostals soon disappeared. Pentecostals generally agreed that while the gift of tongues can be miraculously manifested as an actual language, this is not the normal function of tongues. In keeping with the teaching of Paul, Pentecostals recognized that the normal function of the gift of tongues is the edification of the church through interpretation and as a sign (when interpreted) to unbelievers.

THE EVANGELICAL HERITAGE

For many years Pentecostal bodies shared a common spiritual experience but enjoyed little fellowship or dialogue among themselves. There was even less contact with other Evangelical Christians.[1] Their rejection by fundamentalist dispensationalists on the one hand and the Pentecostal rejection of liberal Protestantism on the other left Pentecostals virtually isolated from the mainstream of American Christianity.

When the National Association of Evangelicals (NAE) was established in 1942, however, that began to change. The NAE brought together a broad coalition of conservative Evangelical Christians who were more representative of traditional Christian orthodoxy than either the rightwing fundamentalists or the left-wing elements of liberal Protestantism.

Many of the major Pentecostal churches were among those invited to join this fellowship. From the outset the NAE saw itself as an alternative to the American Council of Christian Churches (ACCC), a rigid fundamentalist organization headed by Carl McIntire, and the Federal Council of Churches of Christ in America (FCCCA), which served as the voice of liberal Christianity in America. Pentecostals were in the minority of NAE membership during the 1940s and 1950s, but they felt at home with the doctrinal position and social agenda of the Evangelical community.[2] This experience helped Pentecostals discover that their spiritual heritage is in the patristic, Reformation, and post-Reformation traditions, as well as in the Wesleyan-Holiness influences of the American frontier.

Formation of the National Association of Evangelicals was not an attempt to introduce something novel into the life of the church. Its purpose was to restore a heritage of orthodoxy seriously threatened by extremism and the strong currents of modernism. Carl Henry, a leading Evangelical spokesman, defines an Evangelical as "one who believes the evangel." He elaborates on this by saying:

> The Good News is that the Holy Spirit gives spiritual life to all who repent and receive divine salvation proffered in the incarnate, crucified and risen Redeemer. The Christian message is what the inspired Scriptures teach—no more, no less—and an evangelical is a person whose life is governed by the scriptural revelation of God and His purposes.[3]

This would include:

A belief in the doctrine of the Trinity, the two natures of Christ, the Virgin Birth, the bodily resurrection and second coming of Christ, salvation by grace through faith, the sinfulness of man, the sacrificial death of Christ for sin, the Bible as the inspired Word of God and the final norm for doctrine, evangelism as the main task of the church, and the Christian life as one of holiness and godliness.[4]

While Pentecostals had believed and preached these doctrines since the inception of their movement, the spiritual and theological solidarity they found with other Evangelicals helped raise their consciousness of being a vital part of a conservative Christianity. They came to see that their roots could be traced throughout the history of the church.

The Patristic Tradition

Church fathers, whose writings cover the critical period from the death of the apostles to Isidore of Seville (560-636), were the wellsprings of the establishment of Christian orthodoxy. They were the great bishops, teachers, and theologians whose lives and writings were important to the Christian witness at a time when the gospel was particularly susceptible to heresy and misunderstanding. The Christian church is deeply indebted to the Fathers for the many ways in which they contributed to the theological, moral, and spiritual continuity of biblical faith. Through treatises, sermons, commentaries, and practical writings of virtually every description, the Fathers helped establish the foundations for the doctrine and worship of the church. In the brief treatment that follows are noted some of the major contributions of the early church fathers that Pentecostals—and Evangelicals—claim as part of their own spiritual and theological heritage.

The Apostles' Creed

The Apostles' Creed did not exist in its present form before the fifth or sixth century, but its essential core was known to Irenaeus and Tertullian as early as the latter part of the second century. The creed reads:

> I believe in God the Father Almighty, maker of heaven and earth;
>
> And in Jesus Christ his only Son our Lord: who was conceived by the Holy Ghost, born of the Virgin Mary, suffered under Pontius Pilate, was crucified, dead, and buried. He descended into hell; the third day He rose again from the dead; he ascended into heaven, and sitteth at the right hand of God the Father Almighty; from thence he shall come to judge the quick and the dead.
>
> I believe in the Holy Ghost; the holy catholic Church; the communion of saints; the forgiveness of sins: the resurrection of the body; and the life everlasting. Amen.[5]

Next to the biblical canon itself, the Apostles' Creed was the most authoritative criterion for faith in the early history of the Western church. Its importance rested on its antiquity and on its normative content. The Creed served two important functions. It was used for instructing candidates for baptism and as a rule of faith for Christian orthodoxy. The

Apostles' Creed obviously served both of these purposes well, but it did more. It protected crucial evangelical truths from serious heresy in the second and third centuries.

The heresy we refer to is *Gnosticism* (a term derived from the Greek word *gnosis*, meaning knowledge). Many different forms existed; but in the main, Gnosticism was a widespread religious movement representing a mixture of virtually all the religious traditions of that time.

Philosophically, Gnostics were dualists. This means they understood reality to consist of two ultimate principles: matter and spirit. They believed that the created material world is evil and that it was created by an evil god whom Gnostics like Marcion equated with the God of the Old Testament. Salvation or deliverance, for the Gnostic, essentially meant deliverance from the material world through intellectual participation in the divine realm. Since Gnostics believed the salvation of the soul is hindered by the flesh and material things, it was natural for them to believe that the liberation of the divine element within oneself could be hastened by an ascetic life and a mystical knowledge reserved for the spiritually elite. Only those who had been initiated into the mysteries were worthy of participating in this liberating truth.

Gnostics believed that the divine Christ had descended from the spirit world in order to free the souls of men from the evil realm of matter. This divine being united Himself for a time with the person known historically as Jesus of Nazareth, but they did not believe this divine Savior was really a fleshly human being at all. As William Hordern explains:

One group insisted that the divine Christ had adopted the human Jesus for a short time and had acted
and spoken through him, but had fled from Jesus
before the crucifixion. Another group insisted that
Jesus did not really have a body at all; it was a clever
hallucination. Whichever school a Gnostic belonged
to, he agreed in denying that Jesus was in any sense
a true human being. This Christian heresy did not
deny that Jesus was divine; it denied that Jesus was
human.[6]

While most Gnostics rejected outright the Old
Testament, others sought to purge the New
Testament of all the elements they found contrary to
their own mystical philosophy. In addition to under-
mining the true humanity of Jesus, they denied the
goodness of the created order, the value of the body,
the bodily resurrection of Christ, and the importance
of this earthly life. The integrity of the Christian
faith was at risk, and anti-Gnostic Fathers like
Irenaeus, Tertullian, and Hippolytus rose up to meet
the threat.

One of the ways the church addressed the heresy
was through the affirmations of the Apostles' Creed.[7]
The Creed begins by affirming belief in "God the
Father Almighty, maker of heaven and earth." In so
doing, it affirms the creation of the world by the
Father God and not some demiurge, as Marcion had
claimed. In so doing, the Creed also affirms the
goodness of the created order and its value for the
human family. It denies that the Son was some kind
of phantom figure by asserting that He is the Son of
the Creator; and that He, from His conception,
shared man's flesh (that is, was truly human). It

affirms that He suffered and died as any fleshly, historical man would suffer and die. In affirming the "resurrection of the body" the Creed was, at the same time, affirming the bodily resurrection of the Savior and rejecting the view that the body has no real worth. The Creed was organized, as most creeds were, around a Trinitarian affirmation of belief in the Father, Son, and Holy Spirit. To this important issue of the Trinity, we now turn our attention.

The Triunity of God

Evangelical Christians do not accept the authority of the church fathers or the infallibility of ecumenical councils, as Roman Catholics do. As valuable as the teachings of the Fathers and the councils may be, they were not divinely inspired as were the Holy Scriptures. The loyalty of Protestants has always been to the principle of *sola Scriptura*, the authority of Scripture alone. But this should in no way be taken to mean that Evangelicals have a low opinion of the great creeds of the church. On the contrary, Evangelicals recognize the high stake all Christians have in the great historic creeds. As Bernard Ramm, a well-known Evangelical theologian, notes:

> An evangelical who holds an ahistorical faith has no real sense of the theological and spiritual continuity of his faith. The church is the body of Christ, not only for the first centuries but for all centuries. The very concept of the church as the body of Christ implies historical continuity. The unity of the Spirit (Ephesians 4:3) implies the continuity of the Spirit. Having a sense of one's historical roots gives one a

sense of being a member of the body of Christ, the company of believers of all centuries, and of keeping both the unity and the continuity of the Holy Spirit. This sense of continuity—of sharing in a heritage of theology and life, of faith and action—is an integral part of deep Christian conviction. It is having a sense of the Tradition amid traditions.[8]

Many theologians regard the Nicene Creed of A.D. 381 as the best summary of the Christian faith. Most Christians still honor it, along with the Apostles' Creed, as an orthodox formulation of their faith and often recite it in public worship. The special significance this creed has for Christians is that it attempts to answer the most fundamental of questions, "Who is God?" It reads:

I believe in one God: the Father Almighty, maker of heaven and earth, and of all things visible and invisible;

And in one Lord Jesus Christ, the only begotten Son of God: begotten of the Father before all worlds, God of Gods, Light of Light, very God of very God, begotten, not made; being of one substance with the Father, through whom all things were made; who for us men and for our salvation came down from heaven, and was incarnate by the Holy Ghost of the Virgin Mary, and was made man, and was crucified also for us under Pontius Pilate; he suffered and was buried, and the third day he rose again according to the Scriptures, and ascended into heaven, and sitteth on the right hand of the Father; and he shall come again with glory, to judge both the quick and the dead; whose kingdom shall have no end.

And I believe in the Holy Ghost, the Lord, the giver of life, who proceedeth from the Father and the Son,

who with the Father and the Son together is worshiped and glorified, who spake by the prophets.

And I believe in one holy catholic and apostolic
Church: I acknowledge one baptism for the remission of sins. And I look for the resurrection of the
dead, and the life of the world to come. Amen.[9]

The belief that Jesus Christ was indeed God and
that God had acted decisively through the life, death,
and resurrection of Jesus for the salvation of
humankind was the most basic thing New Testament
Christians had been called to believe. But this belief
presented an enormous intellectual problem. While
the church recognized the reality of God in Jesus of
Nazareth and in the work of the Holy Spirit, it shared
with Judaism its monotheistic faith in one God. The
church understood the basic tenets of God's self-dis-
closure. God is one and is not to be understood in
terms of multiple deities such as one finds in pagan
polytheism. The ancient Shema—"Hear, O Israel:
The Lord our God, the Lord is one!" (Deuteronomy
6:4)—was the cornerstone of belief about God for both
Christians and Jews. On the other hand, God had
been revealed as Father, Son, and Holy Spirit. How
could the church affirm both this trinity of persons
and the unity (oneness) of God?

As the church translated its faith into forms of
expression that those outside Jewish culture could
understand, and as it protected its sacred truths
against the constant onslaught of heresies, it found it
necessary to clarify and articulate its thinking about
the nature of God. The long history of the church's
struggle with this question is much too involved to

be retold here, but it came to a climactic watershed at the Council of Nicaea in A.D. 325, and at Constantinople in A.D. 381. In the end it resulted in a great debate between Arius and Athanasius over the nature of the Son and the Son's relation to the Father.

Arius, a presbyter from Alexandria, began preaching that the Son was not eternal but had been created by the Father as an agent of creation and redemption. This forced the church to clarify its thinking about the nature of the Son and the Son's relation to the Father. The Holy Spirit, Arius taught, was in turn a creature of the Son.

Athanasius, bishop of Alexandria, recognized the seriousness of Arius' heresy and vigorously argued against the view that the Son was a lesser deity or creation of the Father. The Son, he insisted, shares the same divine substance (*homoousios*) as the Father. Athanasius also argued that the Holy Spirit is fully divine and shares the same divine nature as the Father and the Son. Athanasius fully respected the mystery of the Trinity, but he also recognized the dangers in remaining silent about so important an issue. If the Son was not fully God, he reasoned, how could God have been fully revealed through the Son? If the Son was not fully divine, then how could we be fully redeemed? Athanasius, the great champion of Nicene orthodoxy, knew that this was no mere speculative matter, but one that affected the very core of salvation itself.

The Nicene Creed contained three major responses to Arianism that all orthodox Christians can appreciate. *First*, it notes that the Son was "begotten, not made." This was in direct response to Arius' teaching and was meant to deny that the Father existed before the Son, or that the Father had in any sense created the Son. What Athanasius and the church fathers wanted to affirm was that the Father and the Son are coeternal and equal in power and glory. It should be noted that the biblical word *begotten* comes from the Greek word *monogenes*, which implies the uniqueness of the Son and that the Father and the Son were "of the same kind or substance."

Second, the Creed affirms outright that the Son is of the same substance (*homoousios*) as the Father. This means simply that the Son is fully God and that He shares the same divine nature as the Father.

Third, the Holy Spirit is described as "the Lord, and giver of life, who proceedeth from the Father and the Son, who with the Father and the Son together is worshiped and glorified, who spake by the prophets." It is significant that the church recognized the Spirit's full divinity, placing the Holy Spirit on the same level as the Father and the Son. The Creed also recognizes the place of the Holy Spirit in the faith and worship of the church. In indicating the procession of the Spirit from the Father and the Son, the church was again emphasizing the coequality of the Father and the Son.

Through this definitive expression of its faith, the church said something fundamentally important about the nature of God. It affirmed the triunity of Father, Son, and Holy Spirit. But just as importantly, it gave successive generations of Christians a basis for their Christocentric faith.

The Person of Jesus Christ

If Jesus Christ is not only central to but also normative for the Christian faith, it follows that the church would inevitably have to ask the question "Who is Jesus Christ?" The doctrine of the Trinity had focused on the unity of God in the context of a faith that had asserted the divinity of the Father, the divinity of the Son, and the divinity of the Holy Spirit. The Christological question, on the other hand, had to do with the relation between the human and divine natures of Christ. How could the church affirm that full humanity and full divinity had been united in Christ?

Against the orthodox position that Jesus Christ was both God and man, four major views provoked serious controversy within the church. *Arianism*, described earlier, denied the full deity of Christ. *Apollinarianism*, on the other hand, denied the full humanity of Christ. Apollinarius taught that when the Word (that is, the *Logos*) became flesh, everything about Jesus remained human except one—His spirit or intelligence. The human Jesus did not, in fact, have a human intelligence but retained the divine intelligence of the Logos. The church reasoned, however, that if Jesus did not have a human spirit He could not be fully human. He would have possessed perfect godhood but lacked complete manhood. And if there was a complete manhood in Christ, how could it be claimed that the whole of human nature had been redeemed?

The issue of how the divine and human natures were conjoined in Christ was taken up by the *Nestorians* and the *Monophysites*. Nestorius, bishop of Constantinople, advanced the view that there were two natures in Christ (the human and the divine) that existed in perfect harmony, but that these natures remained physically distinct. The error of Nestorius was in his denial of the physical union of the two natures into one person. The *Monophysites* (the name comes from the Greek words for "single" and "nature") argued that in Jesus Christ the human and divine natures had been so united that there were no longer two natures in Christ but a single nature that had been deified. In this view, the distinction of the two natures was altogether lost.

While this controversy may seem like unnecessary wrangling, we must recognize the importance of an orthodox position concerning the person of Christ. What the church could not afford to do was to insist on the divinity of Christ without maintaining the full, real humanity of Jesus. The Scriptures were clear that "the Word became flesh" (John 1:14) The salvation of humankind was as dependent on the humanity of Jesus as it was His divinity. The church could in no way deny the full divinity of Jesus, for the Scriptures clearly taught that He was the Son of God. In becoming flesh the Logos had in no way given up the divine nature. He was, and would remain forever, the God-man.

Building on their earlier acceptance of the Nicene Creed, the church affirmed its belief in the union and distinction of the human and divine natures in the one person of Jesus Christ. This affirmation was established in the form of an orthodox Christology at the Council of Chalcedon in A.D. 451.

We, then, following the holy Fathers, all with one consent, teach men to confess one and the same Son, our
Lord Jesus Christ, the same perfect in Godhead and
also perfect in manhood; truly God and truly man, of
a reasonable soul and body; consubstantial with the
Father according to the Godhead, and consubstantial
with us according to the Manhood; one and the same
Christ, Son, Lord, only-begotten, to be acknowledged
in two natures, inconfusedly, unchangeably, indivisi-
bly, inseparably; the distinction of natures being by no
means taken away by the union, but rather the prop-
erty of each nature being preserved, and concurring
in one Person and one Subsistence, not parted or
divided into two persons, but one and the same Son,
and only-begotten, God the Word, the Lord Jesus
Christ; as the prophets from the beginning have
declared concerning him, and the Lord Jesus Christ
himself has taught us, and the Creed of the holy
Fathers has handed down to us.[10]

Original Sin

Augustine (A.D. 354-430), bishop of Hippo, was
the leading champion of Christian orthodoxy during
the patristic period. His *Confessions* and *City of God*
are among the great Christian classics, and his influence on the course of theology for the next 1,000
years can hardly be overstated. His understanding
of Christian truth was not worked out in a peaceful
academic setting but through an ongoing struggle
with the leading heresies of his day.

Against Manichaean dualism Augustine maintained that God was the sole Creator of all things
and that God alone sustains all He has created. Evil
is not explained, Augustine insisted, in terms of an

eternal evil being or agency but as the privation of the good. Against the Donatists, who contended that sacraments conferred by those who were "unholy" were invalid, Augustine taught that the unworthiness of the minister did not affect the validity of the sacraments since their true minister was Christ. Augustine's later years, however, were taken up with the more serious controversy with Pelagius over the issue of original sin.

Pelagius, a British monk living in Rome, taught that Adam's fall had affected no one but Adam. Every person is completely free at every moment of life to choose good or evil. To Pelagius' credit, it should be noted that he did not set out to be a heretic. His aim was to convince morally lax Christians that it was entirely within their power to turn to God and live a holy life. "A Christian," Pelagius said, "is he who is not merely such in name but in works, who in all things imitates and follows Christ."[11] The grace to do that, he believed, had been given through creation, which allowed all to fulfill naturally God's moral demands through the exercise of free will. Doing good is difficult for us only because we have practiced sinning so much. It is the habit or example of disobedience that we pass on to our posterity, not a sinful nature.

Augustine had a different understanding of sin. Human nature, he insisted, has been permanently affected by the sin of Adam. Through Adam's transgression, sin entered the human race and all have come under its power. All of Adam's posterity choose and act according to their sinful nature. They can in no way pull themselves up by their own volitional or moral bootstraps. Apart from the helping grace of God, it is impossible to break out of the bondage of sin and overcome it by one's own free will. Humans have the "freedom to sin" but not "freedom not to sin." This is the essence of original sin, and all are condemned to live under its power until they take on a new humanity in Jesus Christ.

The inherited weakness or inability we have received from Adam, Augustine believed, is the inability to make God the center of our lives. The essence of sin is pride, the centering of one's life in oneself. It is the desire to be free from God. Sin is an unrestrained lust after the world, the flesh, and the devil. In our refusal to make God and His Word the center of our lives, we demonstrate our kinship with the first man, Adam. Because we can in no way heal the deep cause of our sin and restore ourself to a right relationship with God, Augustine concluded, our salvation depends entirely on the grace of God. Augustine was indeed the great "doctor of grace" in the Christian church. For this reason Protestants and Catholics alike claim him as their own.

Augustine's analysis of the human condition, however, led him to conclusions about predestination that were different from the views of many Catholics and Protestants. Since salvation is entirely in the hands of a sovereign God, Augustine reasoned, God must choose, or elect, those whom He wills to save. This aspect of Augustine's thought wielded influence on John Calvin and some of the other Reformers. But Evangelical Arminians, including most Pentecostals, find a closer affinity with those who, while taking original sin seriously and holding that the grace of God must precede the exercise of free will, maintain the capacity of the human will to cooperate with or resist the grace of God.[12]

The Atonement

Virtually all Christians agree that being brought back into "at-one-ment" with God is directly related to the life, death, and resurrection of Jesus. But various views have been put forth as to the nature of salvation and how it is accomplished. Interestingly enough, there has never been an official formulation in orthodox Christianity of the Atonement, as there was for the Trinity and the nature of Christ. But Evangelical Christians have had strong views about the nature of Christ's redemptive work.

For some of the early Apostolic Fathers, including Clement of Rome and Justin Martyr, salvation essentially meant illumination or knowledge. Christ, for them, was the source of enlightenment. He was the example by which one could escape the powers of ignorance and evil, and live according to Christ's enlightened teachings (Acts 26:18). Unlike the Gnostics, who held that a saving knowledge was for only a select few, these Fathers believed that the teaching of the Logos was open for all to know and share. Problems with this view include its truncated view of sin as ignorance and its total misconception of Christ's redemptive work.

The Eastern church tended to think of salvation in terms of deification. Athanasius, in particular, emphasized that as the human soul is restored to God's image, it becomes deified. This is what it means to partake of the divine nature (2 Peter 1:4), he said. The new birth is the beginning of this process and culminates in our being brought into the kingdom of heaven according to His likeness.

This view is typified in Athanasius' saying, "He became man that we might become divine."[13] Athanasius' understanding of redemption is primarily concerned with the restoration and incorruptibility of human nature (that is, the deification of humankind). It has virtually nothing to say about Christ's freeing us from sin and guilt. Sin is understood in terms of mortality, and salvation is understood as the restoration of immortality and incorruptibility. It is, as many have noted, a physical concept of redemption.

Origen, another Eastern theologian, interpreted the Atonement in terms of Christ's great triumph over Satan and the forces of evil. This is often referred to as the ransom theory. In this view, Jesus handed His soul over to Satan in exchange for the souls of humanity. After accepting this exchange, Satan discovered that neither he nor death could hold the sinless soul of the Son of God. Through the power of His resurrection, Christ triumphed over sin and death and provided for the restoration of all things, which were formerly under the forces of evil. Christ's victory was a cosmic victory with universalist implications (Colossians 2:15).

Origen's grand vision of the Atonement, however, was actually part of its deficiency, because it did not relate the work of salvation to individual lives. Nor did it adequately relate salvation to the specific problem of sin and guilt.

Abelard, a medieval theologian, advocated the so-called moral influence theory of the Atonement. In his view the death of Christ was simply a supreme manifestation of God's love. The purpose of this great self-sacrifice was to free humankind from the fear of God and to move the heart toward God through repentance and reciprocating love. This theory said nothing about Christ's death as a satisfaction for sin. Abelard had such a weak view of sin that there was actually little that needed to be forgiven. Our sin essentially consists of our contempt for God's will. Christ's suffering death was meant to shame us out of our waywardness. Abelard's view of the Atonement was never accepted in the mainstream of Christian orthodoxy because it was based on an inadequate view of sin and did not address the problem of a God whose nature had been offended by this sin.

There were, of course, elements of truth in all of these views of the Atonement. But none of them provided an adequate explanation of how we are saved. The view that Evangelicals have found to be most consistent with the teaching of Scripture is the one advocated by Anselm of Canterbury in the 12th century.

In his well-known work on the nature of the Atonement, *Cur Deus Homo* (why God became man), Anselm taught that the death of Christ should be seen as a sacrifice for sin. Christ lived a perfect life and died a death of perfect obedience in order to satisfy the requirements of God's justice. Christ's death was indeed the supreme expression of God's love for fallen humanity, but it was more than self-sacrifice. It was a necessary sacrifice for sin so that we might be saved from the penalty and guilt of our rebellion against a holy God.

Christ was more than a representative of the human race. He was our substitute who died to pay the penalty for our sins so that we might be restored to the favor and image of God. The Atonement rests entirely in the merits of Christ. As Martin Luther emphasized, justification before God does not mean that we ourselves are righteous but that we have been forgiven and accepted as righteous for Christ's sake.

Questions for Reflection

1. Who is an Evangelical? Explain what Evangelicals believe. Why do Pentecostals embrace the Evangelical heritage?

2. What was Gnosticism? Which affirmations in the Apostles' Creed directly refute the Gnostic heresy?

3. What is the attitude of Evangelicals toward the church fathers and the great historic creeds? Why is the Nicene Creed so important? Explain the significance of the great controversy between Arius and Athanasius.

4. What was the great Christological question? Explain the error in the views of Apollinarius, Nestorius, and the Monophysites. Point out specific statements in the Council of Chalcedon (A.D. 451) that refute these errors.

5. What was the critical issue in the controversy between Augustine and Pelagius? On which specific issues do Evangelicals agree with Augustine's position? On which issues do many Evangelicals, including most Pentecostals, differ with Augustine?

6. Explain these views of the nature of the Atonement: illumination, deification, Christ as victor over Satan, moral influence theory, the Atonement as satisfaction for sin. Critique each view and explain why Anselm's view is more biblically sound.

Notes

[1]Many Pentecostal leaders became acquainted with each other first at NAE meetings in the early 1940s. This led to serious discussions about a fellowship among themselves. This fellowship was finally created in 1948 as the Pentecostal Fellowship of North America (PFNA), for the purpose of promoting fellowship and demonstrating unity among Pentecostals.

[2]The rapid growth of Pentecostals in recent years has now moved them into a majority position in the NAE. It is significant that when the PFNA adopted its "Statement of Truth" in 1948, there was only one article that differed from the NAE "Statement of Faith." That was Article 5, which read:

> We believe that the full gospel includes holiness of heart and life, healing for the body and baptism in the Holy Spirit with the initial evidence of speaking in other tongues as the Spirit gives utterance. (Compare with chapters 3 and 4 of this volume.)

[3]Bob E. Patterson, *Carl F.H. Henry: Makers of the Modern Theological Mind* (Waco, Texas: Word Books, 1983), pp. 14, 15.

[4]*Ibid.*, p. 27. With the exception of the dispensationalist emphasis of most fundamentalists, the differences between Evangelicals and fundamentalists are more a matter of attitude and mood than doctrine. What Evangelicals particularly dislike about some fundamentalists is the attitude of separatism, an often negative attitude toward education and scholarship, and failure to apply Christianity to the whole of life, including the social and cultural dimension.

[5]Hugh T. Kerr, *Readings in Christian Thought* (Nashville, Tenn.: Abingdon Press, 1966), p. 75.

[6]William Hordern, *A Layman's Guide to Protestant Theology* (London: Macmillan Co., 1968), p. 12.

7 The Apostles' Creed was a symbol in the early church, and assent to it was required of those receiving Christian baptism. The term symbol, when applied to a creed, means that the creed is a test of membership in the church.

8Bernard Ramm, *The Evangelical Heritage* (Waco, Texas: Word Books, 1973), p. 15.

9Kerr, pp. 75, 76.

10*Ibid.*

11Cited in Bernard Lohse, *A Short History of Christian Doctrine* (Philadelphia: Fortress Press, 1980), p. 109. For good concise treatments of this and other issues discussed in this chapter, see Donald McKim's *Theological Turning Points: Major Issues in Christian Thought* (Atlanta: John Knox Press, 1988).

12This view is closer to that of Ambrose than Augustine. See Kenneth Scott Latourette, *A History of Christianity*, vol. 1 (New York: Harper and Row, 1975), p. 177.

13Cited in McKim, p. 84.

THE
REFORMATION
HERITAGE

During the medieval centuries many changes took place in the church. The patristic church, which had struggled to establish Christian orthodoxy during the formative period of the church's history, eventually gave way to a highly institutionalized Roman Catholic Church that developed a life, liturgy, and theology of its own. During this period of the church's history, the papacy and the hierarchy of the church were institutionalized, the seven sacraments were carefully articulated, and a Marian theology took root. Also during this period, the scholastic method of learning and teaching theology rose to prominence in the newly established universities, and a distinctive form of Roman Catholic piety began to be practiced.

The most serious changes in the church, however, were in doctrines and practices that served to obscure the meaning of the gospel itself. Some examples of these changes were penance, indulgences, and good works. The church slowly but surely made itself the sole ark of salvation and the custodian of God's activity on earth. Martin Luther boldly observed that the Roman Church had tried to turn itself into Christ and had instead become anti-Christ. Men of deep convictions spoke out against the errors and abuses of the church but were silenced or ignored. Reformers (protesters), like Peter Waldo, John Wycliffe, John Hus, and William Tyndale were joined by Martin Luther, John Calvin, and Ulrich Zwingli in a chorus of protest on behalf of the great evangelical truths of the Bible.[1]

At the heart of their reform were those issues that most affected the gospel. They included a return to the authority of Scripture, the priesthood of all believers, the sovereignty of God's grace, and a reconstructed doctrine of the church and the sacraments.

The Authority of Scripture

The rallying cry of virtually all of the Protestant Reformers was "back to the Bible." The church's appeal to its own traditions, which had taken on an authority equal to that of Scripture, moved the Roman Church farther away from the gospel. Before any other issue could be meaningfully addressed, the church would have to decide whether it would listen to the voice of tradition or Scripture. Would the church continue to listen only to its own interior monologue and conform itself to its own traditions and vested interests, or would it listen to the voice of God speaking through His Word? The formative principle of authority would have to be settled before the church could deal with other matters of theological substance.

Early Christians inherited a deposit of faith and patterns of life from the apostles which dated back to the teachings of Christ. These doctrines and life patterns drew their supreme authority from Old and New Testament Scripture which was known and available from the second century. At first this authority was not in opposition to the oral tradition, which also went back to the apostles. The church recognized that the gospel had been transmitted in both written and oral form, so they did not see Scripture and tradition opposed to each other.

The adoption of the New Testament Canon, however, raised important questions about the tradition. Since heretics like the Gnostics could also appeal to Scripture and to their own version of the tradition, the church felt it necessary to have an official version of Scripture and tradition. This meant that the church would have to designate its own official interpreters of the Bible and the tradition. Since bishops in the church had come to be regarded as the successors of the apostles, it seemed natural for them to have teaching authority in the church and be the official interpreters of all matters pertaining to doctrine and morals. The church could then claim that it had an authoritative apostolic canon of Scripture and an authoritative apostolic rule of faith.

The church was soon claiming, however, that this apostolic rule of faith was not derived from the New

Testament but that it existed prior to the biblical Canon and was meant to be a guide to the interpretation of the Bible. This was an unfortunate error, for the Roman Church was soon exalting its own authority above that of Scripture. The church reasoned that since it had vested the Canon with authority, the church itself was the higher authority and the ultimate rule of faith. With the church in possession of both an authoritative apostolic doctrine and a permanent apostolic office, individual believers had essentially been denied the privilege of hearing and interpreting the Word of God.

As the Roman Church increased in size and power, its hierarchy came to regard the institutional church as the church Christ established. Primacy, it taught, was promised and bestowed on the apostle Peter, who became the first bishop of Rome. Peter and his apostolic successors would head the church as the earthly representatives of Christ until the end of time. Their teachings, whether in ecumenical councils or dispersed throughout the world, would be regarded as authentic and infallible.

Medieval Catholicism did not reject the authority of Scripture; it simply held that Scripture and church tradition were complementary truths. Augustine gave early approval to this coauthority when he stated: "I could not believe the Gospel, unless the authority of the Catholic church moved me."[2] For all practical purposes, the die was cast for the next 1,000 years. The relationship between Scripture and church tradition in the Middle Ages can be described as subordination of the former to the latter.

This subordination of Scripture to tradition was encouraged by the gradual elevation of the papacy above the other bishops. From the time of Gregory the Great (590-604), the chair of Peter increased in power and authority to the point that Boniface VIII (1294-1303) took the final fateful step. He likened his power to that of the sun and stated unequivocally in a papal bull (*Unam Sanctam*, 1302) that "subjection to the Roman pontiff is absolutely necessary to salvation for every human creature." The subsequent rise of nation-states, the secularizing influence of Renaissance humanism, and the Enlightenment tended to temper the power of the papacy; but the Roman Church continued to reaffirm its rule of faith in the church and the pope.

At the Vatican Council of 1870, the church defined the doctrine of papal infallibility, which declared that when the pope speaks *ex cathedra* (from the seat of authority), he possesses "that infallibility with which the divine Redeemer willed His church should be endowed for defining doctrine regarding faith or morals." (The Second Vatican Council in 1959 placed greater emphasis on biblical studies and the church's spiritual and invisible character but did not reform its rule of faith. It simply moderated papal monarchy in favor of greater emphasis on the shared authority of all the bishops.)

Against this background the Protestant Reformers insisted on the principle of *sola Scriptura* (Scripture alone) as the only true basis for doctrine and morals. This Protestant principle repudiates the idea that Scripture needs any authority other than its own.

It is important to be clear about where Catholics and Protestants agreed and disagreed on the matter of biblical authority. Both held that the Bible embodies a supernatural revelation and that it is authoritative for Christians. The major point of disagreement, as Paul Tillich points out, was how Roman Catholics and Protestants believed that we are related to God. Catholics held that since the Scriptures were deposited with the church on the people's behalf, the church must mediate and authenticate these teachings by its testimony. Tillich calls this "a system of divine-human management, represented and actualized by ecclesiastical management."[3] Protestants, on the other hand, held that the only ultimate authority for Christians is the message of the gospel and this message can be directly addressed to the individual through the Scriptures without the mediation of the church. Thus, Protestants offered a relation to God that was personal, basing it only on the message of God's gracious acceptance of the sinner in Jesus Christ.

The Protestant Reformation was born out of Luther's personal spiritual experiences, which he found without the church's mediation. When he returned to the Bible, he did not find the authority of the church. He found, instead, the freedom of the Christian life through Paul's doctrine of justification by faith alone. The Bible was for Luther the "carpenter's ruler," the "proof stone," the standard to which all reason, experience, tradition, and church doctrine had to conform. Scripture alone is to be believed and trusted. With this wine no water is to be mixed; alongside this sun no lantern is to be held. The Spirit did not reside in popes, in canon law, or in councils. The Spirit, Luther argued, is inseparably united with the Word. Luther took his stand on Scripture. "My conscience," he said during his most trying time, "is held captive by the Word of God."

But Luther found more than a rule or source of authority in Scripture. He found a living faith. The Spirit, Luther believed, resided in the Word. There could be no Spirit without the normative Word. But neither could there be a living faith without the Holy Spirit. Luther found the Bible to be a living authority which made itself felt and heard through authentic religious experience.

Since the authority of Scripture is the formative principle upon which Protestant theology is built, one may rightfully ask what, precisely, is it that Protestants believe about the Bible. *First, Protestants set the authority of the Scriptures above the church or any other alleged authority.* The church did not give birth to the Scriptures; rather, the Word of God (especially, the gospel) formed the church. The church does not give itself the Word of God. It can only recognize and acknowledge the divine inspiration and authority that is inherent in the Word. As Bernard Ramm notes, "It is the Word of God which nourishes, feeds, and sustains the church. The church may well be the custodian of Scripture, but it is Scripture that rules the custodian and not the custodian who rules Scripture. The church is not to be the lord and master of the Scripture, but Scripture is to be the critic of the church."[4]

Second, when Protestants speak of the Scriptures, they do not include the so-called Apocrypha or Pseudepigrapha as part of the Old Testament Canon.[5] They include only those books that comprised the Jewish canon of the Old Testament. Protestants do not discard the other books, because they recognize their historical and cultural value, but they do not believe the *Apocrypha* and *Pseudepigrapha* possess the same level of inspiration as the 39 books that comprised the Jewish canon of Scripture.

Third, Protestants hold that the Scriptures carry their own self-authentication and their own clarity. The Bible is not the Word of God because the church declares it to be but because the Word validates itself. As the roar of the lion validates the fact that the lion is a lion, and the majesty of a king reflects his kingship, the power and majesty of the Word authenticates itself.[6] Similarly, the Word carries within itself its own clarity. One does not have to look to the church to know the right meaning of Scripture. One can, Luther insisted, know the literal meaning of Scripture by applying the principles of grammar and sound interpretation. Humanistic scholarship, however, is not enough. One must understand the spiritual or internal clarity of Scripture through the work of the Holy Spirit. The thematic clarity of Scripture, Luther insisted, is Jesus Christ. He is the unity, harmony, and substance of Scripture to which everything else leads. Scripture is complete in itself. Passages which are obscure must be understood in the light of the total teaching of Scripture on any subject. In this way no part of Scripture may clash with the teaching of the whole.

Protestant Reformers recognized that one of the gravest errors of the Roman Catholic Church had been to make itself the teacher. By vesting all teaching authority in the bishops, Rome depreciated the importance of the Spirit's inner witness and illumination of the Word in individual believers. The

Reformers attempted to correct this error by returning to the Holy Spirit as the only true and infallible Teacher. God uses Scripture to make His will known, but the Holy Spirit gives life and meaning to the words.

There was, however, an extreme position on this issue that was equally dangerous. There were radical reformers whose extreme emphasis on their experience of the Holy Spirit led them to believe they had no need of external authorities or teachers. Many of them felt they did not need the church at all—or even the written Word—for they had the Holy Spirit to teach them. Their claim of private interpretation and spiritual guidance led these ultra-Protestants to scorn all authorities and the need for sound learning and clear doctrine. This was an opposite extreme that the Reformers stood ready to combat also.

The Reformation placed importance on learning and the role of the teacher. But the understanding of that role was greatly modified by Protestant principles. The teacher was no longer regarded as an infallible interpreter, like the magisterium of the Catholic church. The teacher was a learned believer capable of biblical exegesis and an application of the teachings of Scripture. The teacher has no right of private interpretation but rather the duty of constantly reexamining and teaching the church's doctrines. Church teaching and tradition, the Reformers said, must constantly be examined in the light of Scripture. Reform is never finished; it is an ongoing activity in the life of the church.

This principle led Protestants to affirm the importance of both sound learning and church councils. The internal witness of the Spirit does not cause one to abandon mind or reason. Mature belief requires the full consent of one's faculties. If we are to know and believe what God has revealed, we must apply ourselves to learning and a knowledge of the Word. This is not intellectualism or anti-intellectualism; it is the necessary union of Word and Spirit.

The right and liberty of everyone to interpret and judge is a privilege fraught with danger. Fanatical and carnal individuals often rise up and boast presumptuously that they know the Spirit's will for the church. To guard against this danger, doctrine must have its public as well as its private test. The public test refers to the common consensus and polity of the church. It is necessary for the faithful to meet together and seek a basis for agreement. This is the purpose for general assemblies and councils of the church. Solomon said, "Where there is no counsel, the people fall; but in the multitude of counselors there is safety" (Proverbs 11:14). Assemblies of holy men and women are more than so many heads and opinions. Even in diversity the Holy Spirit can bring forth unity and essential agreement on essential matters.[7]

On the basis of sound biblical principles, the Protestant Reformers established key practical principles to govern their doctrine of *sola Scriptura*. They included

1. A healthy regard for the mind and reason as well as the internal witness of the Holy Spirit

2. The necessity of learned teachers, preachers, and laypeople who can understand and rightly divide the Word of God

3. An unabashed necessity for sound theology in the life of the church (not on the periphery but in the center of the church's life)

4. An ongoing need in the church for reexamination and wise counsel.

The Priesthood of All Believers

Martin Luther and John Calvin were great scholars as well as preachers and reformers. Luther translated the Bible from the original languages into the German vernacular so that "every schoolboy," he said, could be armed with Scripture. John Calvin published his first edition of the *Institutes* when he was only 26. He spoke of his great work on theology as a Bible study—as an aid to students in reading the Scriptures. Luther and Calvin knew the meaning of loving God with one's mind as well as with one's heart. Their scholarship was motivated by their consciousness of every believer's need for studying and learning the Word of God. Neither the teacher nor the learner has the right of private interpretation, but all may rightfully participate in the ongoing reexamination of the faith of the church.

The medieval church viewed itself not only as the ark of salvation but as the supreme authority on earth as well. It did not hesitate to assert its authority in matters concerning politics, economics, morals, or theology. Priests in the church were the special class through whom the church exercised its authority, particularly its sacerdotal authority. Priests were called the intercessors between God and humankind. The church taught that it was the only authority God had duly established to dispense grace and teach the truths of God, and priests were the special class through whom this grace and knowledge was mediated.

Luther felt compelled to challenge the church's mediatorial role. He had found the basis for a right relationship to God through the scriptural teaching of justification by faith alone, and was convinced that through Christ every Christian could be his or her own priest before God. Jesus Christ is the Great High Priest; and by following His pattern and offering themselves up to God, every believer can share in this priesthood.

Breaking with the recognized religious authorities of the church which everyone had been taught to accept, however, was one of the most agonizing decisions Luther had to make. How could he hope to stand alone against the whole world of official Christendom?

Fundamental truth gave Luther the courage to take his stand. He knew his own experience of God had not been mediated through the church. The content of this experience was "justification by faith," which Luther described as being accepted by a righteous God on the basis of Christ's merits alone. This was no heavenly mystery that required a specialized unraveling or articulation by the official clergy. It was truth a simple plowboy, armed with Scripture, could understand. Luther's conviction concerning the basic clarity and plainness of understanding Scripture motivated him to recover the Bible from the hands of the priests and place it in the hands of the people. The truth of Scripture had to be wrested away from the institutional church. To achieve this, Luther dedicated himself to the task of

translating the Bible from the language of the scholars (Latin) to the language of the people (German).
He also determined to abandon the old allegorical
method of reading the Bible, which depended on the
church's interpretation, in favor of a grammatico-his-
torical principle of interpretation by which the text
would speak for itself.

Accepting Scripture as the rule of faith, Luther
found he could then support his experience against
the ecclesiastical authorities. Together, the witness of
Scripture and experience could establish the truth of
Christ which the institutional church had lost. What
gave rise to Luther's break from Roman authority
was not the mere fact of the Bible but the message of
Christ which Luther found when he turned to the
Bible. The certitude of faith and Scripture offered a
far greater certainty than any the institutional church
could provide.

When the Reformers said that all Christians are
priests and have access to God, they did not mean
that priesthood is private or individualistic.
Individual priesthood did not mean individualism.
There was no intent on the part of the Reformers to
place the locus of attention on the isolated individual. Spiritual gifts are bestowed on individuals for
the good of and the building up of the whole body of
Christ (1 Corinthians 12; Ephesians 4:11, 12). Caring,
bearing, sharing, and loving are all a part of the
social and communal character our priesthood must
assume. The Holy Spirit brings the individual
believer into right relationship with God so that he
or she can be baptized into Christ's body. The grace
of God cannot be institutionalized so that the church
can control and dispense it at will. On the other

hand, grace is "the grace of our Lord Jesus Christ" and therefore cannot be privatized. It belongs to Him and His purposes for the body.

Belief in the priesthood of all believers carried with it important implications for the Protestant church. For one thing, it tended to do away with the old medieval distinction between "sacred" and "secular" callings. Luther believed God could be served equally well in any vocation or calling. All of life belongs to God and should not be divided into sacred and secular realms. It is not necessary to be a monk in a monastery to be in full-time Christian service. One can just as well offer his or her full-time Christian service and praise to God in the kitchen, at the cobbler's bench, or driving an oxcart. All callings from God are sacred and should be treated as such. As Luther put the matter:

> What you do in your house is worth as much as if you did it up in heaven for our Lord God. For what we do in our calling here on earth in accordance with His Word and command, He counts as if it were done in heaven for Him. . . . Therefore we should accustom ourselves to think of our position and work as sacred and well-pleasing to God, not on account of the position and the work, but on account of the Word and faith from which the obedience and the work flow. No Christian should despise his position and life if he is living in accordance with the Word of God, but should say, "I believe in Jesus Christ, and do as the Ten Commandments teach, and pray that our dear Lord God may help me thus to do." That is a right and holy life, and cannot be made holier even if one fast himself to death.[8]

There is one essential priesthood in the church—

the ministry of Jesus Christ. All believers are called to share in that ministry. There are many forms of ministry, but the same Spirit inspires all of them (1 Corinthians 12:4-7). The intent of the Reformers in tearing down the old distinction between sacred and secular callings was not to bring down the office of the priest or minister but to elevate to their proper place the callings of ordinary people. Robert McAfee Brown explains the New Testament perspective:

> In the New Testament, *laos* (laymen) does not mean church members who are non-clergy. It means everybody. *Kleros* (clergy) does not mean church members who are in a special category. It means everybody. Both words are used in the New Testament, but they are used to describe the same people, the whole *people* of God.

> If we examine the New Testament word for "ministry," *diakonia*, we are led to a similar conclusion. Originally, *diakonia* (from which our word *deacon* derives) meant waiting on tables (cf. Luke 17:8). It gradually came to mean one who serves others, one who ministers. In the early church everything that led to the building up of the Christian community was *diakonia*—service, ministry. Every Christian participated in this *diakonia*, so every Christian was a servant, a minister.[9]

This does not mean that every ministry was the same, for some in the New Testament church were specifically called to give themselves to prayer and the Word. Churches coming out of the Reformation tradition recognize that some are especially called and ordained for the ministry of the Word and the sacraments, but they also understand that the ordained ministry is only a part of the ministry of the whole people of God, who are rooted in the priesthood of Jesus Christ.

Justification by Faith Alone

Martin Luther was a Roman Catholic priest with a deep sense of his own sinfulness. His guilt was no doubt aided by the kind of piety that had become common in the late Middle Ages. Great emphasis was placed on the physical sufferings of Jesus and the role of the Father as a vengeful Judge. Pietas showing the dead Christ in the arms of Mary and pictorial representations of His "bleeding heart" were everywhere. A God who was angry with sinners and was soon to unleash His wrath and judgment on them was a constant theme in medieval art and the preaching of the church. To the guilt-burdened Catholic, the practice of penance took on special importance.

The common belief was that one could be set right with God, or "justified," by doing things pleasing to God. One could, for example, become a monk, go on a pilgrimage, mortify the flesh, fast, say special prayers, give a special offering to the church, or do any number of things that could lead to favor with God. Luther tried to justify himself before God by doing all of these things, but he only felt more guilty and frustrated. Like the servant in the Bible who concluded, "We are unworthy servants; we have only done our duty" (Luke 17:10, *NIV*), Luther never felt he had done enough. In a word, his dilemma was trying to find the approval of a righteous and holy God. How could he gain God's acceptance?

Works didn't work. Was there any other way to gain the love and favor of a righteous God?

When Luther turned to Scripture he found the answer to his problem. It was, in fact, a problem he could do nothing about because God had already done everything. In Jesus Christ, God had already provided the basis for His acceptance of sinners. Christ did not lay down His life for worthy people; instead, He "demonstrates His own love toward us, in that while we were still sinners, Christ died for us" (Romans 5:8). Our salvation depends entirely, Luther discovered, on the grace of our Lord Jesus Christ (John 1:17; see also Acts 15:11). God will never love or accept us more, regardless of anything we do or don't do, than He already does in Jesus Christ. God's relationship to us is unlike any relationships we know about or experience. It is a personal one based entirely on God's gracious acceptance of us in Jesus Christ. Robert McAfee Brown beautifully illustrates the point:

> Some human relationships are based on merit: a baseball club employs a player because he can hit .340 or is exceptionally adept with a glove. Some relationships are based on need: I get acquainted with a garage mechanic because he can fix my broken carburetor, or I get acquainted with a banker because he can help me stay solvent. Some relationships are based on appeal: a man does not love a woman because she can fix his carburetor or help him stay solvent, but because he finds her beautiful, or appealing, or exciting to be with.

> The relationship based on grace is unlike the relationship based on merit or need or appeal. God

does not enter into personal relationship with His children because they are "good." They are not. Nor does He do so because He "needs" them. He does not. He is not gracious to them because they are "appealing." They are not. Quite the contrary. The Bible is emphatic in asserting that God's relationship to man is not based on the fact that man offers something to God, but on the fact that God offers everything to man.[10]

All we can do is trust in what God has already done. Faith is having the courage to accept the fact that in Jesus Christ we have already been accepted. In accepting that fact we find mercy and forgiveness, and this becomes the basis for all right relationships. Having been forgiven and accepted by God, we can now forgive and accept ourselves and others. In Christ we find power to live the Christian life. "I have been crucified with Christ," Paul said in Galatians 2:20; "it is no longer I who live, but Christ lives in me; and the life which I now live in the flesh I live by faith in the Son of God, who loved me and gave Himself for me" (Galatians 2:20). This is the gospel, the "good news" that the Protestant Reformers recovered from the Word of God.

The fact that we receive this grace as a free gift does not mean it was cheap. As Dietrich Bonhoeffer emphasized in *The Cost of Discipleship*, the grace of our Lord Jesus Christ cost God everything. The cost of this grace was the Cross. God has freely given us Himself through the Son that we might have abundant and eternal life. There was no way that this salvation could have been earned by good works, but this does not mean that good works are unimportant to God. God has indeed saved us *for* a life of good works. They are the fruit of our salvation. "Good works do not make a good man," Luther said, "but a good man does good works."[11]

A Reconstructed Doctrine of the Church and Sacraments

One of the major concerns of the Protestant Reformers was to recover the life and vitality of the church in light of the gospel of grace. In Catholicism, the "church" always meant the visible institutional church of Rome, which saw itself as the dispenser of grace, the place where Christ's presence is celebrated, and the possessor of the keys of heaven. The church considered itself to be one piece, like the garment of Christ. To the church there was no legitimate way it could be cut asunder. When the Reformation created a schism within the church, Rome could only regard it as a rending of the body.

The church also regarded itself as a mixed body. The Lord allows the wheat and tares to grow together and allows both good and bad fish in the same net until He returns to make the separation. Until then both good and bad people were expected in the church. The church did not view itself as a separated people or a holy community.

The Roman Church was essentially a hierarchy of power that was believed to mirror heavenly realities. At the top of the heavenly realities was the triune God; at the top of the institutional hierarchy was the pope, the representative (vicar) of Christ on the earth. Following the pope on a descending scale were the cardinals, archbishops, bishops, priests, and finally the faithful laypeople. The means of grace, received through the sacraments, moved from the top to the bottom of the pyramid.

Everything about the system served to suggest the distinction between official clergy and the faithful. Late in the medieval period, the idea emerged that church councils were better representatives of the faithful than the pope. Those who espoused this view, the conciliarists, were never able to overcome the earlier emphasis on papal supremacy and the entrenched hierarchical structure of the church.

Following the lead of Luther and Calvin, Protestants were critical of Rome's identification of the gospel with everything spoken by the institutional church. Where Roman Catholics understood God to be present with His people through the church, Protestants understood God to be present through the Word and sacraments of the gospel. What the Reformers wanted most was to reestablish the sovereignty of Christ over His church. "Wherever you see this Word preached, believed, confessed, and acted on," Luther said, "there do not doubt that there must be a true holy catholic church . . . for God's Word does not go away empty."[12] Similarly, Calvin wrote: "Wherever we see the Word of God sincerely preached and heard, wherever we see the sacraments administered according to the institution of Christ, there we cannot have any doubt that the Church of God has some existence, since His promise cannot fail, 'Where two or three are gathered together in My name, there am I in the midst of them.'"[13] The Reformers made the gospel of Christ central to everything else. They aimed to reform the old church by the Word of God.

This inevitably changed the image of the church and its operation. The Reformers removed the hierarchy from the church and replaced the sacerdotal office of the priest with the concept of the "priesthood of all believers." For the sake of church order, Protestant congregations continued to call gifted pastors and teachers to fill the offices of the church. They continued to see that pastors were properly trained for their task, but ordination ceased to have sacramental meaning or be an exalted position in the Protestant tradition. The minister was regarded as simply a servant of the Word he proclaims. His primary responsibilities were to preach the Word and administer the sacraments. He was no longer expected to be celibate but could marry. He was no longer standing above the people but with them. His primary responsibility was to open the Word of God so that it could be clearly heard and understood by all.

The minister's effectiveness and success did not depend on his personal charisma but on the faithfulness of God to His covenant promises given through the Word and the sacraments. The pulpit became the central focus in Protestant churches, and the sermon became the central act of the worship service. Laypeople were given more participation in the worship service through the singing of hymns, the reading of the Word, and full participation in the sacraments.

The Reformation was four movements, not one—though all four were vitally related in spirit and doctrine. There were the Lutheran and the Calvinistic branches, the Anglican movement in England, and the so-called radical or left-wing groups on the continent and in England. The latter included such diverse groups as the Anabaptists, Baptists, Congregationalists, Quakers, Mennonites, and various other smaller groups. What distinguished these smaller groups from the mainstream of the Reformation was their view of the church. Philip Schaff, church historian, put this distinction in perspective: "The reformers aimed to reform the old church by the Bible; the radicals [Anabaptists] attempted to build a new church from the Bible."[14]

The Anabaptists envisioned a literal return to the original simplicity of the New Testament church. They did not want a church built on the model of Rome, Wittenberg (Luther), or Geneva (Calvin). Their model was the early church at Jerusalem as a community of saints separated from the world.

In the minds of Luther and Calvin, the fall of the church had been due to a corrupted theology. What needed to be restored was the truth of the Word and the proper administration of the sacraments. The Anabaptists, on the other hand, believed that the greatest need of the church was for it to follow the pattern of Christ. New Testament Christianity was more than faith and doctrine; it was a commitment to follow the ways of Christ. Discipleship was not something connected to the ecclesiastical church (as Rome prescribed), nor was it something idealized or spiritualized like the Reformers' view of the invisible church. It was conformity to the life and character of Jesus Christ. The Anabaptists believed that the church must have a visible form—visible to itself and to others—but that this form had to be shaped by the New Testament pattern of Christian living.

Anabaptists imaged the church as a group of believers gathered together by the Holy Spirit for the purpose of being a Christian community in the world. The church was a voluntary nonpolitical reality that was totally separate from the state. The only way one could be a part of the true church was through the inner transformation of the new birth and an outward following of Christ. Most Anabaptists emphasized at least four aspects of discipleship:

- Obedience to the Great Commission
- A life of love and nonresistance
- A willingness to suffer in the spirit of cross bearing
- A separated life of holiness[15]

Anabaptists rejected totally the idea of a territorial or state church. In place of an institutional church connected to the state, the Anabaptists emphasized peoplehood and the importance of corporate individuality. They reasserted the biblical role of the laity and the local congregation. They stressed the importance of serving one another in love and being a disciplined community of saints in the world. Infant baptism, as practiced by Catholics and mainline Protestants, was a contradiction to all that Anabaptists believed. In fact, the name *Anabaptist* literally means "rebaptizer," a reference to the fact they "rebaptized" those who had received infant baptism—on the grounds it was no baptism since infants could not exercise their own faith. Anabaptists were cruelly persecuted by Catholics and other Protestants for their beliefs and their lifestyles. Many were martyred.

The Reformation led to an almost total dismantling

of the Catholic sacramental system. Lutheranism rejected the Catholic doctrine of transubstantiation, which held that during the Lord's Supper the bread and wine miraculously become, in substance, the body and blood of Christ. Luther's view was that the body of Christ was literally present in the mind of the believer when the Supper is taken in faith, but that the bread and wine coexist in union with each other without being changed (a view known as consubstantiation). Although he held to a slightly different view than Luther, Calvin also believed in the real presence of Christ in the Supper and that the believer receives an infusion of divine grace through the sacrament.

It was Ulrich Zwingli, a Swiss Reformer, who offered a really different view of the Lord's Supper. Zwingli emphasized Jesus' admonition "This do in remembrance of Me" as the key to interpreting the meaning of the Supper. Sacraments, he believed, are essentially symbolic. They remind us of Christ and the significance He has for us. They are commanded so that believers may continually identify with and contemplate Him. Water baptism is our first and decisive identification with Christ. Through baptism we identify with His death and resurrection. In the Supper we continue to identify with Him as we confess His name, remember His death, and anticipate His return. Many of the Anabaptists also washed feet because it was practiced by Christ and His disciples, but they did not raise this practice to the level of a sacrament.

Post-Reformation Movements

Classical Protestantism rediscovered the Bible and many biblical truths that had been lost or obscured for centuries. It was as though the church had emerged out of a long, dark tunnel into the light of a new day. But one would be in error to assume that the Reformers disavowed all continuity with the past or depreciated the importance of the witness from the Catholic tradition. How could they forget the witness of the church's martyrs, or the courageous manner in which the early apologists had defended the faith? They did not overlook the contribution the monasteries and abbeys had made to learning, or the fact that the early ecumenical councils had struggled with the Trinitarian controversy (Nicaea, A.D. 325) and the problem of the two natures of Christ (Chalcedon, A.D. 451) and had formulated creedal statements to which they as Protestants were still committed. They could not forget the intellectual achievements of great theologians like Augustine, Anselm, Bonaventure, Lombard, Abelard, and Aquinas. Nor could they forget the mystical devotion of Bernard of Clairvaux, Francis of Assisi, Catherine of Siena, and Thomas à Kempis. Those faithful Catholics who had tried to reform the church but whose voices had been silenced could never be forgotten.

Reformers also realized that while they had recovered important biblical doctrines and practices, there were others which they had not recovered or had recovered only in part. Under new circumstances and newly inspired insights, the Reformers fully expected the spirit of reform to break out again and again. With Scripture as the source and test of faith, they encouraged the church to follow the principle *Ecclesia reformata sed semper reformanda*—the church reformed but always to be reformed. Many reforming groups would follow this principle in the post-Reformation era.

The Reformation was born through Luther's experience of justification by faith and his reflection on that experience in the light of Scripture. Later in his life, however, Luther moved away from the experiential side of faith and placed greater emphasis on faith as right thinking about the truths of the Bible. The original spirit of Luther and Calvin was further betrayed as their successors tended to harden the theology of Protestantism into fixed forms of orthodoxy—correct belief—and scholasticism, where faith was essentially a matter of assent to truth in propositional form. Control of the church by the civil government did not help the situation. The state was always more concerned with intellectual assent to the faith than it was with personal piety and devotion.

The response to this tendency in Lutheranism was pietism, a movement led by Philipp Spener, August Francke, and Count Zinzendorf, whose primary aim was not to make Christians more learned but more pious. Pietists studied the Bible for its edifying and practical benefits. They emphasized the internal testimony of the Holy Spirit and believed that regenerate people can understand Scripture better than the unregenerate. Justification should lead to godliness, and godliness, in turn, should result in the edification of the regenerate. The Holy Spirit received fresh attention among the Pietists as the bearer of renewed life and revitalized feelings.

Most Pietists remained loyal to the Lutheran state church because they were more interested in the invisible nature of the church than they were in its visible forms.[16] Prayer, the study of Scripture, and the reading of devotional literature were the common practices of Pietists when they met together for worship and edification. Their aim was not to repudiate the institutional church but to call for further reform in its moral and spiritual character.

Purity of life and ethical behavior were also dominant themes among Calvinistic communities in England and America. There had always been more emphasis on a disciplined church community in Calvinism than there was in Lutheranism. Puritans were intent on purging all vestiges of Catholicism from the Anglican church in England. Puritans believed in the binding authority of the Bible. They believed that self-discipline, shunning worldly pleasures, and a positive attitude toward work and industry were outward signs of one's inward spiritual and moral condition. Puritans believed in an experienced grace and tended to individualize their relation to God much more than earlier Calvinists. Some even spoke of an experience of "assurance" as a second and subsequent work of the Holy Spirit in the Christian. The Christian life, they believed, was a pilgrimage (e.g., Bunyan's *Pilgrim's Progress*) involving constant warfare. The weary pilgrim triumphs and reaches the heavenly city by bringing all of life under the ordering activity of God.

In worship and polity Puritans rejected the episcopal form of church order in favor of a more democratized form of church government. They believed the episcopal form of church order hindered the vitality and purity of faith as practiced in the New Testament church. The Puritan influence was strong in several denominational groups (Presbyterians, Congregationalists, and Baptists) and was carried to colonial America, where it played an important role in the new experiment with democracy.

The Reformation Influence on Pentecostals

Karl Barth, a highly regarded theologian of the 20th century, remarked on the occasion of his 80th birthday that "there are no great theologians, only theologians who are obedient to the Word of God." In the spirit of Barth's remark, it can be honestly said of Pentecostals that they have historically aspired to be faithful and obedient to the Word of God. No individual or religious movement has a private claim on God's truth. Wherever the gospel is proclaimed, Christians are free to seek truth from it.

Pentecostals, like other religious groups, cherish their doctrinal distinctives. But they realize that these distinctives draw their real significance from the fact that they are grounded in the great affirmations of Scripture that were lifted up by the Protestant Reformers. For this reason they proudly join other Evangelicals in claiming the major tenets of Protestantism as part of their own spiritual and theological heritage.

Classical Protestantism, represented by Luther and Calvin, rests on two principles central to Pentecostal belief. The formal principle is the absolute authority of Scripture as the rule of faith. Yet, this principle does not rule out the subjective element involved in the Holy Spirit's work of renewal. He enlightens the believer so that the Word of God may be rightly understood. The material principle is the doctrine of justification by grace through faith. The Holy Spirit gives believers the grace to accept the message of the gospel: through Christ their sins have been forgiven, and those who repent are accepted by a righteous and holy God. The assurance of this justification, as Luther believed, is renewed as the believer returns to the Word and the Lord's Table and discovers there the continuity of God's grace.

Pentecostals find a special spiritual kinship with the Anabaptists and Pietists, however, on several important matters. They endorse the Anabaptist view of adult baptism and Zwingli's view of the Supper. They agree that true biblical faith must manifest itself in a Christlike pattern of New Testament living. This includes the practice of foot washing as well as water baptism and the Lord's Supper. They also embrace the view of the Pietists and the Puritans that genuine faith must pass from biblical attestation into personal experience. This calls for a theology of a new birth whereby the believer can experience the Spirit's work in regeneration. The assurance of this saving grace can be experienced again and again as the indwelling Spirit makes Christ real and present to the believer.

Pentecostals have a special appreciation for the Protestant doctrine of the priesthood of all believers, because salvation by faith obviously has to do with the faith of the individual and the duty of individuals to judge and interpret religious matters for themselves. This does not mean ungoverned individualism but a priesthood for others that follows the pattern of Christ. Pentecostals follow the Anabaptists and some of the more extreme Protestant groups, however, in pushing the priesthood of believers to its logical conclusion in the separation of church and state. They see the church as a voluntary nonpolitical reality gathered by the Holy Spirit. It has both a visible and an invisible character and is composed of all who have truly been born again and who follow Jesus Christ.

Questions for Reflection

1. Explain the Roman Catholic view of the apostolic rule of faith and how it influenced the view that Scripture and tradition are complementary truths. What was the significance of the Protestant claim of *sola Scriptura?*

2. Can you explain what Protestants believe about the Bible in terms of its authority and the Canon? Its self-authentication and clarity? How does a Reformation attitude toward the Bible affect one's view of the Holy Spirit as Teacher? How does it affect one's view of scholarship and learning, theology, and the role of assemblies and councils of the church?

3. What does belief in the priesthood of all believers entail? How does it affect one's belief about the Bible, the church, secular and sacred callings, and ministry to others?

4. Describe Martin Luther's struggle with guilt and condemnation. How did his discovery of the biblical doctrine of justification by grace through faith minister to his personal need? What is the psychological and theological value of this doctrine for all believers?

5. How did the Reformation view of the church differ from the Roman Catholic view? How did their views of the sacraments differ?

6. Who were the Anabaptists, and how did they differ from Luther and Calvin with regard to their views on the church, discipleship, and water bap-

tism? Are Pentecostals more spiritually akin to Anabaptists than to Lutherans and Calvinists on these important matters?

7. Who were the Pietists and the Puritans? What were their essential beliefs, and how were they different from mainline Lutherans and Calvinists? In what ways are Pentecostals indebted to these traditions?

8. Summarize what you believe to be the enduring influence of the Protestant Reformation on the Pentecostal tradition.

Notes

[1]The word *protestant* is a positive term, not a negative one. It comes from the Latin *protestari*, which means "to testify on behalf of" or "to affirm" some strongly held conviction.

[2]Arthur McGiffert, *A History of Christian Thought*, vol. 2 (New York: Scribners, 1961), pp. 114, 115.

[3]Paul Tillich, *A History of Christian Thought* (New York: Simon and Schuster, 1968), p. 228.

[4]Bernard Ramm, *The Evangelical Heritage* (Waco, Texas: Word Books, 1973), p. 26.

[5]The *Apocrypha* includes those books received by the early church as part of the Greek version of the Old Testament, but not included in the Hebrew Bible. The *Pseudepigrapha* refers to those writings ascribed to someone other than their real author for the purpose of giving them an enhanced authority. The term has special reference to those pseudonymous Jewish works dating from the centuries immediately before and after the beginning of the Christian era. These works were not included in the Greek canon of the Old Testament.

[6]Calvin in particular placed great emphasis on the self-authentication of Scripture. Reformed theologians often used the term *autopistos* (credible within itself) and *axiopistos* (worthy of belief by reason of its own inherent worthiness) to describe the majesty of the Word.

[7]Augustine wisely advised Christians that they do not have to agree on everything. He suggested the maxim "In essentials unity, in nonessentials liberty, in all things charity."

[8]Cited in Robert McAfee Brown's *The Spirit of Protestantism* (New York: Oxford University Press, 1965), p. 109.

⁹*Ibid.*, pp. 102, 103.

¹⁰*Ibid.*, p. 55.

¹¹*Ibid.*, p. 65.

¹²See Wace and Bucheim's edition of *Luther's Primary Works*, vol. 12, p. 42; vol. 26, p. 108. Also, see Article 7 of the Augsburg Confession.

¹³*Institutes*, IV. i. 9.

¹⁴Cited in Guy F. Hershberger, ed., *The Recovery of the Anabaptist Vision* (Scottdale, Pa.: Herald Press, 1972), p. 119.

¹⁵*Ibid.*, pp. 135-151.

¹⁶Pietists, for the most part, were not separatists. With the exception of the Moravians, who were led by Zinzendorf, the Pietists remained loyal to the Lutheran state church.

IN
CONCLUSION

In 1958, liberal theologian Henry Van Dusen wrote an article for *Life* magazine in which he described the rapidly rising Pentecostal Movement as "The Third Force in Christendom." The phrase caught on, and it soon became common to call the movement the "third force" and to place Pentecostals alongside Roman Catholics and Protestants as leaders in Christendom.

The "third force" designation was meant to be a compliment to the growth and vitality of the Pentecostal/Charismatic Movement. It emphasized the spiritual benefits that large numbers of people were experiencing because of its spirituality and doctrine. While Pentecostals felt gratified that other Christians had finally begun to recognize the viability and vitality of their movement, there was something about the "third force" designation that made them uncomfortable. They did not think of themselves as an alternative form of Christianity—as a "new force" in Christendom—but as a latter-day continuation of that original work of the Holy Spirit that early Christians knew and experienced in the New Testament. The heritage Pentecostals have always claimed is one that defines its center in Jesus Christ and the fulfillment of His mission in the world through the presence and power of the Holy Spirit.

Pentecostals believe and proclaim a full-gospel message of salvation, sanctification, healing and spiritual gifts, the baptism in the Holy Spirit with the evidence of speaking in tongues as the Spirit gives utterance, and the premillennial second coming of Jesus Christ. With other Evangelical Christians, Pentecostals affirm the classic Christian creeds and are committed to them. Pentecostals believe in God's special work as Creator and preserver, the reliability and authority of Scripture, the sovereignty of God's grace, and the evangelization of the world. They are firmly rooted in the Reformation doctrines of justification by faith alone, the priesthood of all believers, a biblical understanding of church and sacraments, and obedience to the life pattern of Jesus Christ.

Pentecostals, however, do not live in the past. They have an appreciation for the past and for their rich spiritual heritage, but they believe that the Holy Spirit equips us to live with a genuine openness to the present and the future. Meaningless change and uncertainty characterize our times, causing humans to lose the true spiritual center of life. Traditional values and institutions have been undermined in virtually every area of life, but the Holy Spirit is the eternal Spirit. He is the power of the present and the future, as well as the past. There is no need to escape to an idyllic past nor live in fear or dread of an uncertain postmodern future. A sovereign God has fully equipped Spirit-filled Christians to meet the demands and challenges of these times, and He holds the future in His hands.

The new life of the future has already broken into the present through the power of the Holy Spirit. Those living in the life-giving power that raised Jesus from the dead already know the reality of the power of the age to come. Our future is as secure as God's presence and power. We have Jesus' assurance that the Spirit is with us until the end of the age.

The forms through which we express our faith may change with time. The methods through which we minister to the needs of a dynamic society may alter with circumstances. But the message and the power will forever remain the same.

Church of God
Declaration of Faith

We believe

1. In the verbal inspiration of the Bible.

2. In one God eternally existing in three persons; namely, the Father, Son, and Holy Ghost.

3. That Jesus Christ is the only begotten Son of the Father, conceived of the Holy Ghost, and born of the Virgin Mary. That Jesus was crucified, buried, and raised from the dead. That He ascended to heaven and is today at the right hand of the Father as the Intercessor.

4. That all have sinned and come short of the glory of God and that repentance is commanded of God for all and necessary for forgiveness of sins.

5. That justification, regeneration, and the new birth are wrought by faith in the blood of Jesus Christ.

6. In sanctification subsequent to the new birth, through faith in the blood of Christ; through the Word, and by the Holy Ghost.

7. Holiness to be God's standard of living for His people.

8. In the baptism with the Holy Ghost subsequent to a clean heart.

9. In speaking with other tongues as the Spirit gives utterance and that it is the initial evidence of the baptism in the Holy Ghost.

10. In water baptism by immersion, and all who repent should be baptized in the name of the Father, and of the Son, and of the Holy Ghost.

11. Divine healing is provided for all in the Atonement.

12. In the Lord's Supper and washing of the saints' feet.

13. In the premillennial second coming of Jesus. First, to resurrect the righteous dead and to catch away the living saints to Him in the air. Second, to reign on the earth a thousand years.

14. In the bodily resurrection; eternal life for the righteous, and eternal punishment for the wicked.

Suggested Readings

Chapter 1

Bowdle, Donald N., ed. *The Promise and the Power.* Cleveland, Tenn.: Pathway Press, 1980.

Burgess, S.M., et al., eds. *Dictionary of Pentecostal and Charismatic Movements.* Grand Rapids: Zondervan, 1988.

Conn, Charles W. *Like a Mighty Army.* Cleveland, Tenn.: Pathway Press, 1977.

____. *Where the Saints Have Trod.* Cleveland, Tenn.: Pathway Press, 1959.

Cox, Harvey. *Fire From Heaven: The Rise of Pentecostal Spirituality and the Reshaping of Religion in the Twenty-first Century.* New York: Addison-Wesley Publishing Co., 1995.

Dupre, Louis, and Donald E. Saliers, eds. *Christian Spirituality: Post-Reformation and Modern.* New York: Crossroad, 1989.

Gause, R. Hollis. *Living in the Spirit: The Way of Salvation.* Cleveland, Tenn.: Pathway Press, 1980.

Land, Steven J. *Pentecostal Spirituality: A Passion for the Kingdom.* Sheffield, England: Sheffield Academic Press, 1993.

Lemons, Frank W. *Our Pentecostal Heritage.* Cleveland, Tenn.: Pathway Press, 1963.

Chapter 2

Alford, Delton. *Music in the Pentecostal Church.* Cleveland, Tenn.: Pathway Press, 1967.

Boer, Henry. *Pentecost and Missions.* Grand Rapids: Eerdmans, 1961.

Buckalew, J.W. *Incidents in the Life of J.W. Buckalew.* Cleveland, Tenn.: Church of God Publishing House, circa 1920.

Crews, Mickey. *The Church of God: A Social History.* Knoxville, Tenn.: University of Tennessee Press, 1990.

Ellis, J.B. *Blazing the Gospel Trail.* Cleveland, Tenn.: Church of God Publishing House, circa 1941.

Hauerwas, Stanley. *Resident Aliens.* Nashville: Abingdon Press, 1989.

Hughes, Ray H. *Church of God Distinctives.* Cleveland, Tenn.: Pathway Press, 1968.

Jackson, Joseph E. *Reclaiming Our Heritage: The Search for Black History in the Church of God.* Cleveland, Tenn.: Church of God Black Ministries, 1993.

Johns, Cheryl Bridges. *Pentecostal Formation.* Sheffield, England: Sheffield Academic Press, 1993.

Lauster, Bobbie. *Herman Lauster—One Man and God.* Cleveland, Tenn.: Pathway Press, 1967.

May, F.J. *The Book of Acts and Church Growth: Growth Through the Power of God's Holy Spirit.* Cleveland, Tenn.: Pathway Press, 1990.

Synan, Vinson. *The Holiness Pentecostal Movement in the United States.* Grand Rapids: Eerdmans, 1971.

Thomas, John Christopher. *Footwashing in John 13 and the Johannine Community.* Sheffield, England: Sheffield Academic Press, 1991.

Villafane, Eldin. *The Liberating Spirit: Toward an Hispanic American Pentecostal Social Ethic.* Grand Rapids: Eerdmans, 1993.

Chapter 3

Bowdle, Donald N. *Redemption Accomplished and Applied.* Cleveland, Tenn.: Pathway Press, 1972.

Cannon, William. *The Theology of John Wesley.* Nashville: Abingdon-Cokesbury, 1946.

Dayton, Donald W. *Theological Roots of Pentecostalism.* Grand Rapids: Zondervan, 1987.

Gause, R. Hollis. *Living in the Spirit: The Way of Salvation.* Cleveland, Tenn.: Pathway Press, 1980.

Outler, Albert C. *Theology in the Wesleyan Spirit.* Nashville: Discipleship Resources-Tidings, 1975.

Synan, Vinson. *The Holiness Pentecostal Movement in the United States.* Grand Rapids: Eerdmans, 1971.

———. *Aspects of Pentecostal-Charismatic Origins.* Plainfield, N.J.: Logos International, 1974.

Wesley, John. *A Plain Account of Christian Perfection.* London: Epworth Press, 1979.

Williams, Colin W. *John Wesley's Theology Today.* Nashville: Abingdon Press, 1979.

Wynkoop, Mildred Bangs. *Foundations of Wesleyan-Arminian Theology.* Kansas City, Mo.: Beacon Hill Press, 1967.

Chapter 4

Arrington, French L. *The Acts of the Apostles: An Introduction and Commentary.* Peabody, Mass.: Hendrickson Publishers, 1988.

Black, Daniel L. *A Layman's Guide to the Holy Spirit.* Cleveland, Tenn.: Pathway Press, 1988.

Cross, James A. *A Study of the Holy Ghost.* Cleveland, Tenn.: Pathway Press, 1973.

Gause, R. Hollis. *Living in the Spirit: The Way of Salvation.* Cleveland, Tenn.: Pathway Press, 1980.

Gee, Donald. *Concerning Spiritual Gifts.* Springfield, Mo.: Gospel Publishing House, 1972.

Horton, Stanley. *What the Bible Says About the Holy Spirit.* Springfield, Mo.: Gospel Publishing House, 1977.

Horton, Wade H., ed. *The Glossolalia Phenomenon.* Cleveland, Tenn.: Pathway Press, 1966.

McGee, Gary B., ed. *Initial Evidence: Historical and Biblical Perspectives on the Pentecostal Doctrine of Spirit Baptism.* Peabody, Mass.: Hendrickson Publishers, 1991.

Sims, John. *Power With Purpose: The Holy Spirit in Historical and Contemporary Perspective.* Cleveland, Tenn.: Pathway Press, 1980.
Triplett, Bennie S. *A Contemporary Study of the Holy Spirit.* Cleveland, Tenn.: Pathway Press, 1970.

Chapter 5

Arrington, French L. *Christian Doctrine: A Pentecostal Perspective,* Vols. 1-3. Cleveland, Tenn.: Pathway Press, 1992-94.

Bettenson, Henry, ed. *Documents of the Christian Church.* New York: Oxford University Press, 1967.

Bloesch, Donald G. *Essentials of Evangelical Theology,* Vols. 1 & 2. New York: Harper and Row, 1979.

Henry, Carl F.H. *God, Revelation and Authority,* Vols. 1-6, Waco, Texas: Word Books, 1976.

Kerr, Hugh T., ed. *Readings in Christian Thought.* Nashville: Abingdon Press, 1966.

Lohse, Bernhard. *A Short History of Christian Doctrine.* Philadelphia: Fortress Press, 1980.

Marsden, George M. *Reforming Fundamentalism.* Grand Rapids: Eerdmans, 1987.

McKim, Donald K. *Theological Turning Points: Major Issues in Christian Thought.* Atlanta: John Knox Press, 1988.

Ramm, Bernard. *The Evangelical Heritage,* Waco, Texas: Word Books, 1973.

Seeberg, Reinhold. *History of Doctrine.* Grand Rapids: Baker, 1978.

Woodbridge, John A., et al. *The Gospel in America: Themes in the Story of America's Evangelicals.* Grand Rapids: Zondervan, 1979.

Chapter 6

Althaus, Paul. *The Theology of Martin Luther.* Philadelphia: Fortress Press, 1981.

Bainton, Roland. *The Reformation of the Sixteenth Century.* Boston: Beacon Press, 1952.

Brown, Robert McAfee. *The Spirit of Protestantism.* New York: Oxford University Press, 1965.

Calvin, John. *Institutes of the Christian Religion.* (John T. McNeill, ed.; Ford Lewis Battles, trans.). Philadelphia: Westminster Press, 1960.

Dillenberger, John, and Claude Welch. *Protestant Christianity.* New York: Scribner's, 1954.

Hardern, William E. *A Layman's Guide to Protestant Theology.* New York: Macmillan, 1969.

Henry, Carl F.H., ed. *Basic Christian Doctrines.* Grand Rapids: Baker, 1979.

Hershberger, Guy F., ed. *The Recovery of the Anabaptist Vision.* Scottdale, Pa.: Herald Press, 1972.

Schaff, Phillip. *The Creeds of Christendom: Vol. 3, The Evangelical Protestant Creeds, With Translations.* New York: Harper and Brothers, 1877.

Williams, George H. *The Radical Reformation.* Philadelphia: Westminster Press, 1962.